Lines of
Flight

*An
Atomic
Memoir*

Julie Salverson

**WOLSAK
& WYNN**

Cover images: istock (sky with birds), shutterstock (airplane)
Endpaper image: "Iwai Island, Japan, 2015" © Peter C. van Wyck
Cover and interior design: Marijke Friesen
Author photograph: Bernard Clark
Typeset in Minion Pro
Printed by Ball Media, Brantford, Canada

The publisher gratefully acknowledges the support of the Canada Council for the Arts, the Ontario Arts Council and the Canada Book Fund.

Wolsak and Wynn Publishers Ltd.
280 James Street North
Hamilton, ON
Canada L8R 2L3

Library and Archives Canada Cataloguing in Publication

Salverson, Julie, author
    Lines of flight: an atomic memoir / Julie Salverson.

Includes bibliographical references.
ISBN 978-1-928088-25-7 (paperback)

1. Atomic bomb—Japan—Hiroshima. 2. Radioactive substances—Canada, Northern. 3. Nuclear warfare—Social aspects—Canada. I. Title.

D767.25.H6S34 2016   940.54'2521954   C2016-904665-6

For Sharon Rosenberg and Roger Simon.

FOREWORD

To love. To be loved. To never forget your own insignificance. To never get used to the unspeakable violence and the vulgar disparity of life around you. To seek joy in the saddest places. To pursue beauty to its lair. To never simplify what is complicated or complicate what is simple. To respect strength, never power. Above all, to watch. To try and understand. To never look away. And never, never, to forget.
– Arundhati Roy, *The Cost of Living*

The book you now hold in your hands is a curious object. I know this to be true because I was there from the beginning. And in this particular beginning – at least the way Julie tells it – I was on the other end of the phone; she in Kingston, and I on a payphone in the basement of Library and Archives Canada. Having recently seen Peter Blow's documentary *Village of Widows*, I had become obsessed by a piece of "marginal Canadian history" that was at the time almost completely unknown. This film revealed a long and painful story beginning with a uranium mine known to some as Port Radium in the far North of Canada. This material moved over lake, portage and river to the railhead in northern Alberta to a uranium processing plant in Port Hope, Ontario – the "Town that Radiates Friendliness" – and into the maw of the Manhattan Project and its horrific culmination in Hiroshima and Nagasaki. The documentary then returns to the community of Déline on Great Bear Lake, the "Village of Widows." As I stood there on the payphone, I was trying to persuade my new friend and colleague that these were stories we needed to understand, to work with and to tell. Stories from the highway of the atom, as we would call it – of apologies and the Dene, of myths and secrets, of monuments and archives, all circling around Canada's involvement in the great atlas of calamity that was the twentieth century's history with the atom. I knew full well that I needed to be more than one, but less than a crowd – I needed a companion. Somehow, she agreed. And so it was that we set out on the atomic highway.

From the beginning we had thought we would write a book together, but our collaboration was to take us in other directions. And indeed, our collaboration was itself rather unusual. A kind of parallel play, as instructional books on parenting might put it, but this is not exactly right. While it is true that we have never written this book we imagined – although I suspect we will – what we have done is invent a kind of research and field practice where we travel and talk and take notes. And listen. We began to give public readings together, choreographing our words into dialogues. Now when I speak to an audience alone, sometimes when I reach the end of a thought or a passage, I find myself pausing, waiting for the sound of Julie's voice. *What would* she *say here?*

I think we have become witnesses...for each other.

I guess the thing that has bound us together, in addition to the generosity and respect that arose from our friendship-research methods, is the growing archive of our experiences doing this work – the stories, the documents, the images and places. But all of these things, shared though they were, managed to provoke quite different responses from each of us. I found myself writing a somewhat unconventional academic book, *The Highway of the Atom*, while Julie spent nearly a decade writing a clown opera, *Shelter*, and now this book. Julie's footprints are everywhere in my book, though I rarely mention her by name. On the other hand, my name – just a footprint by other means – is everywhere in this book. It is a strange and disembodied feeling to read about this character called "Peter."

Julie calls this book an atomic memoir. But also lines of flight. This, to my academic ear, signals more than the promise of a multitude of stories, of a narrative in flight. In this I hear whispers of the work of the great Parisian storytellers Deleuze and Guattari – *lignes de fuite*. Sometimes this is translated as *lines of escape*, but the important thing is that it calls forth a very different range of meanings from the English sense of the word *flight*. In addition to flying or evading, it evokes the sense of leaking or receding into the distance, as with a vanishing point in a distant landscape. To write, they say, "is to trace lines of flight which are not imaginary, and which one is indeed forced to follow, because in reality writing involves us there, draws us in there. To write is to become." *Lines of Flight* suggests then many possible routes and becomings: approaches, encounters, leading outward, shifting, sometimes askew, receding into a landscape, leaking.

Memoir, on the other hand, while also lifted from the French, draws us into a very different set of movements and routes moving backwards through time. Irradiated and unstable, this memoir is a complex piece of recollection and testimony. To read it is to understand how memory itself is as much aligned with painting as with digging. It is itinerant and peripatetic, moving and creating, connecting and composing, gathering and, above all, gleaning. Picking up the bits. Seeking the remains – the phantoms that secretly animate our lives and families; the traumas that bind us to our work and the worlds we inhabit; and all the invisible routes through which the atomic age becomes intelligible (could this possibly be the right word?) as a *way of life*. Our life.

This book that you now hold in your hands rises up against the bewilderments of time and its oblivions, and against all of the culturally ratified modes of false memory that threaten to foreclose thought and understanding, forgiveness and justice. *Lines of Flight* is an ecology of moments arrested, moments stilled against the backdrop of a world in turmoil. Through a mode of poetic attention, it patiently attends to the silences and gaps. As Don McKay has put it, "some ideas" – or stories, or songs, I would add – "have deep resonance; they reach back into the memory to bring glimmerings, premonitions, intimations into sudden clarity, as though, with their own entry into consciousness, they had simply supplied the candlepower to actually light the bulb."

This book knows that "genuine memory must … yield an image of the person who remembers." It is wise and risky, filled with ravens and sunlight, ghosts and tall tales. It is a guidebook for life in the twenty-first century, an atlas of the wondrous and the wounded. It is also an exercise in a kind of writing that seeks a form equal to the freight of its stories. No easy task. Drawing a line from the brittle kitchens of youth, through the Cold War's reverberations in Canada, to the toxic legacies of the long and convoluted atomic highway, it gathers together the victims and perpetrators, archives and stories, seeking sites of resonance and affinity, exposure and vulnerability. The author is a shape-shifter: a playwright, a dramatist and artisanal storyteller. A trickster, a tourist and ethnographer. A philosopher and (or because) a clown.

All of this is here, in the now, in this careful writing. Through it we find the enigmatic projection of a life – the image of a questioned life.

Peter C. van Wyck
Montréal
June 2016

ONE

I grew up listening to other people's secrets. Vicarious suffering helped me weep. Joseph Campbell says to "follow your bliss," and while others respond by pursuing love or fulfillment, I'm drawn to tragedy and the fault lines in the psyche of a culture – the secrets that fester within families, leak quietly into communities and sometimes explode. When I was in grade nine, some friends let my mother and I stay alone in their cottage on Georgian Bay. One night she went to sleep with candles burning. I was in my usual spot, out on the rocky cliff watching the stars. I came back around midnight to burning curtains. We drove home in silence to our small village outside Toronto. My parents talked quietly in the kitchen about a trial separation – between me and my mother's drinking.

Dad was packing for Montreal to spend a few months writing a science fiction television series, so I went to live with a neighbour. Sylvia's old farmhouse was calm and I loved chatting with her while she made dinner. I admired her graceful hands as she taught me to chop garlic. "Vigorous, be vigorous!" she said, standing back to coach as I pressed hard on the flattened knife.

Sylvia treated me like an adult. She had been a dancer in her youth and now helped young women get abortions by driving them across the American border. I thought this secret rescue operation was even more glamorous than ballet. Sylvia did something in the world about real problems. Not like the neurotic dramas at our house. Perhaps that was when I decided to become an activist and save the world.

"What goes on with your parents isn't your fault," she assured me. "You'll be an adult soon, everything will be fine. You'll be fine." Her tanned face crinkled when she smiled. I think Sylvia really believed that growing up would offer me refuge.

Now, in my forty-sixth year, my life has imploded. There are no visible wounds or outward signs, but I have lost my compass. I have lost faith in my own life and I don't know why. I see little value in my work. I have no idea how to be a good daughter to my widowed father. I am too busy to see my friends. Nobody can count on me, not even myself.

As exhaustion draws me deeper into the winter of 2001, I stop answering emails or returning calls. I don't have it in me to be a responsible citizen. This is a crisis of identity, a challenge to my picture of myself. I have spent my life trying to save the planet. In my teens there was God, in my twenties, political activism. Now there is nothing.

One Saturday morning, while huddled over coffee, I notice a headline on the pile of newspapers that have collected on my kitchen table. "The Day the Sky Exploded" announces scientists have discovered all there is to know about what happened when an atomic bomb fell on Hiroshima. It was almost sixty years ago; time to close the book and move on. One sentence in particular catches my eye: "All uncertainties must be ironed out."[1] I laugh. I haven't thought consciously about nuclear weapons for ages, but this pristine image of closure strikes me as so ridiculous, my own unravelling feels comforting by comparison. For a moment, I'm glad to be as confused as most people I know. Certainty makes me nervous; I'm not easily reassured. I'm the person who hears something like this and buys a plane ticket to Japan.

I throw on jeans and a T-shirt and search the bathroom for some skin cream. My face in the mirror is strained, tight lines around my eyes daring me to pay attention.

The phone rings. Shit.

I recognize the name on the call display and answer. I don't know Peter van Wyck very well, but I like him. We'd met a year earlier when he applied for a position at my university, Queen's, in Kingston. I'd listened to his calm and thoughtful presentation and was intrigued. With none of the bravado or name-dropping that often occurs, his scholarship was powerful poetry about nuclear threat and test site contamination. He got the job and we were drawn together by our common interest in stories of violence. We cooked up a course to co-teach, but he was subsequently head-hunted for a more permanent position with Concordia University, and he and his wife moved to Montreal. I had no expectation that we would stay in touch. Why was Peter calling me on the weekend?

"I have a crazy idea for you," he says. "Do you want to hear it?"

"Sure." What the hell. Little did I know that this would be the proverbial cliché, the phone call that changes one's life. So much so that I can't remember what it was *not* to know what Peter was about to tell me. Or not to know Peter.

His voice is a deep baritone. "Did you know that the uranium used to develop the atomic bombs dropped on Japan came from a uranium mine in northern Canada?" No, I didn't. Nor did most people, I would later learn. Somehow this was left out of our public school curriculum. I glance again at the article on my table, the name Hiroshima jumping out at me, and tell him to keep talking.

"The mine was shut down in the sixties," he says, "but the site is still there, on the edge of Great Bear Lake, in the Northwest Territories. It's about five hundred kilometres north of Edmonton, near a town called Déline. I have this idea that maybe we could take a trip."

The opening lines of a play I wrote flash through my head: "What would you do," a teacher asks a student, "if I told you something you don't want to know?" The student thinks. "I guess it depends what happens after you hear a bad story. Do I have to feel bad?" The teacher smiles. "Oh, you'll feel bad when you hear about this!" I feel like hanging up the phone before Peter says any more. What horrors is he about to reveal? What is the connection between uranium on a lake in northern Canada and Hiroshima?

Peter has called me because for most of my life I have worked with survivors of trauma. I've written and made plays about it. What he doesn't know is I don't want to do this anymore.

In my work with survivors of violence – refugees, victims of assault, marginalized youth – they tell me their experiences and we create a play. I become their witness. Meeting people under these circumstances is never dull and helping them stage their experiences is rewarding, even pleasurable. What isn't fun is listening to accounts of abuse, aggression and cruelty. Perhaps this was the source of my exhaustion. What kind of person pursues trauma like a thrill-seeker chasing storms and then agonizes over not being able to help? I once told my therapist I couldn't do anything for a friend going through cancer. "All I can do is listen." My therapist shook his head. "You think listening is a small thing?"

I've never believed that listening was enough. What do I *do* with what I hear? I didn't grow up with organized religion, but my father would tell stories about how his Icelandic grandfather in Winnipeg carried food to other new immigrants. They lived in tents by the Red River at forty degrees below zero. The city had organizations in place that the old Icelander could have worked with, but that wasn't my great-grandfather's way. You didn't trust charities or groups to do your job for you. You paid attention and rolled up your sleeves.

On the day that Peter called, I had decided I needed a break from anything to do with trauma. I'd sent out a kind of force field announcement to the universe: "Enough is enough!" Of course when you do that kind of thing the opposite tends to happen. But I had a legitimate reason. I was following professional advice.

My acupuncturist's office is a corner suite at the end of a luxurious hallway of old oak and refurbished copper. One week before Peter's call, I was face down on a table beside a large window. Outside, geese splashed in a river overflowing from the previous night's rain. My acupuncturist is German. She is competent and kind, and her white coat sparkled in the sunshine. I winced as each needle entered my aching back. "You are exhausted," she said.

I told her that I had come back from Germany a month earlier. "I've been tired and listless ever since."

"You haven't fully returned," she murmured. "Your physical body is here but not your ethereal body. Part of you is still over there, the part that isn't yet finished with the journey. What were you doing in Europe?"

I sighed into her lavender pillow. This sounded new age to me, but to say I was not "all there" felt accurate. "I work as a playwright with people who've survived trauma. I help them tell their stories. I've been visiting memorials and museums about the Holocaust."

There was a pause as strips of paper were efficiently ripped from needles. She plunged them into the bottom of my spine.

"This treatment will make you feel better. Help you return. But it is not enough."

Geese honked frantically. She strode to the window and slammed it shut. "Next time, you must study something else." I felt a gentle hand on the back of my neck. "Next time, why don't you research paradise?"

A week later, standing in my kitchen with the phone in my hand, I don't want to hear any more. I'm pretty sure that if Peter says one more thing I'm going to be stuck with this story. It's clear to me that knowing just a bit about something leading from a relatively obscure corner of Canadian history to the dropping of the atomic bomb will not be good enough. If I keep listening, this phone call will become the beginning of a very long trip. We will attempt to follow a path of stories, rethink the meaning of directions and instructions, walk forward and stumble back. We will leave a lot behind and get very, very lost. I consider hanging up. But, inevitably, I stay on the line and he tells me that when the Dene found out about the connection between their land and the bomb, ten of them got on a plane and went to Japan to offer the *hibakusha* – the survivors – an apology.

"Will you come with me?" Peter shouts as the connection breaks. "Shall we take a trip along this highway of the atom and see what happens?"

"Sure thing," I mumble, though the truth is I'm horrified. It doesn't seem like the kind of hike someone should take alone.

Two months later, Peter and I are in his Montreal office writing a grant proposal to the Canadian government. We want to follow the path of Canadian uranium and its stories, and write about what it means to bear witness to a route, an historical account and an archive. Our biggest question is about the apology: What kind of responsibility are they taking, these Dene from northern Canada, who surely are victims in this situation and not perpetrators?

As I draft my pages I am conflicted. How did my acupuncturist put it? *Next time, why don't you research paradise?* Shouldn't I be finding hopeful stories to write about, not flying to a uranium mine, and to a community that has lost many of its elders to cancer?

I state reasons why I must do this project: I can be a witness; I can write about it; I have a track record as a scholar and playwright. I've become too good at generating ideas – they rush out in a torrent of explanation. Do I really want to immerse myself in another disaster? Like an addict I type furiously – arguments, rationales, possibilities. I print the pages and admire their tidy lines, the smell of fresh ink.

I pore over scholarship and writing that inspires me, framing my part of the research proposal in terms of what it means to bear witness to historical memory. I find a spiral notebook from graduate school and read a passage I have written and underlined heavily. It comes from an ethics class taken with my supervisor, Roger I. Simon: "In Jewish tradition, there is the path (*haggadah*) and the law (*halakhah*). *Halakhah* is from the root *halakh*: to walk, to go. It is about what is binding, commanded, permitted, forbidden. The *haggadah* is from the root *higgid*: to say, tell, narrate. It is about stories, legends and witticism. The path is not something followed; it is something transmitted, passed on, listened for. It is dangerous when the requirement to pass on is forgotten. Or lost."

I am not Jewish but this tradition captures something important. What path am I meant to follow, and how can I know I am making the right decision? In the classical world one sought help from a high priest, the augur, who interpreted the signs, the movement of the stars and the paths of birds. When we lose our bearings, our ability to read the signs of our lives, how do we find our way back to our path, our lines of flight?

Suddenly I have a gut sense that this trip might be just what the doctor ordered. For once the destination is my own country, but it's more than that. I have been obsessed with nuclear war and atomic bombs all my life; maybe it's time I ask why. I decide to write my way through my own haunting. I won't only travel the path of Canada's connection to the atomic bomb. If I'm lucky, I'll unravel my own.

TWO

There's a photo of me from when I'm six. It's an October day in 1961 and I'm lying in the backyard dirt with my neighbour Stacey. She lived across the street and was a bit of a mystery. I wasn't in her class; we weren't even at the same school. In the picture we're both covered up to our shoulders in leaves. Stacey has short blonde hair and a white T-shirt, both features washed out by the black-and-white Brownie camera snapshot. She grins and leans back as she tosses a pile of leaves up above her head. Nothing falls into her hair or eyes; handfuls of what I imagine are reds and golds float, a crown about to descend. I am closer than her to the camera. Brown curls frame my face; my eyes are fixed on my friend. I'm the youngest, but I'm the one on guard.

For as long as I can remember it's been my job to protect those I love. Growing up our house was often filled with my parents' show business friends, usually wildly interesting and spectacularly drunk. After the crowds departed my parents were left facing only each other, and their exuberance turned to rage. My mother finished those evenings sobbing in the kitchen while Dad retreated to his office with his harmonica. I would then take command of my younger brother, grab blankets and pull him down the hill to the barn. While I brushed the sleek coat of my bewildered horse, Scott sat sombre and responsible with his BB gun, keeping the barnyard safe. Without his vigilance rats would come in the night and drag the baby ducklings down their holes.

My mother started telling me secrets when I was twelve. I came home from school one day to find her weeping uncontrollably in the kitchen. An old family friend had died – my father's best friend. I held the Kleenex box and squirmed as she confessed that this man had been her secret lover. "The love of my life," she whispered. As I held her and stroked her back, my mother calmed down. "I can always depend on you," she sighed. It was a lesson I took to heart. I would be rewarded for taking away my mother's pain. I was proud to be her confidant.

Another secret she revealed regarded a first husband I hadn't known existed. He was a pilot during World War II. I could hardly imagine this, my mother with another man, not my father, both not yet twenty. It made my already glamorous actress mother something more private, more mysterious. She'd had another life, a boyfriend she dreamed about while still in school – someone who would be torn from her, taken by the war. I listened, thrilled, to what she told me. He might have died, her life marked by tragedy. I wanted her to tell me this was how it ended. But no, the story was simpler and, to my teenage sensibilities, sadder.

Mom married when she was nineteen. She lived with the boy, the pilot, for a few months and then he was gone. She told me he had trained at the Royal Canadian Air Force base near Trenton. She thinks she waved goodbye to him there sometime in 1942.

One year later she broke up with him by sending him a Dear John letter. My mother wanted to join the CBC and become a radio actress, and she didn't know how to do that and be married to a stranger at the same time. I was fourteen when she told me all this, my beautiful mother crying while navigating downtown Toronto traffic in our new white Datsun. "I felt so terrible," she kept saying.

A year after this confession my mother received a letter. The pilot had survived, had a family of his own. I think he taught elementary school. She took me aside in our kitchen after dinner and told me she was planning to meet him and that I mustn't tell my dad. I don't think he would have minded, but Mum needed something special, her own secret. Or maybe she needed my father to care.

That same weekend I went on the one and only date of my high school life, with Dave, a bucktoothed grade eleven student who told bad jokes and laughed at them himself. Maybe he was just nervous. We saw Norman Jewison's *Fiddler on the Roof*. I was sorry the movie was long as I'd have to listen to more jokes in the intermission. While we stood in line for popcorn at the University Theatre on Bloor Street I saw my mother and her first husband – it must have been him, who else could it have been – in the back corner of the lobby, heads together, whispering. I hadn't ever seen her look like that with my dad. I never told her that I was there, or that I had seen the movie.

When I was sixteen I started going to seminars about how to survive nuclear war. It was 1971 and the peace movement – the one my generation thought would save the world – was just getting going. Helen Caldicott hadn't yet terrified us with her documentary *If You Love This Planet*, but still I didn't sleep at night. While my parents sat with their scotches watching *The Ed Sullivan Show* on our black-and-white television, I went to the field behind our house to see if planes flying overhead would drop something big. I lived in perpetual anticipation of sudden explosions. I wanted to be sure that when the world blew up there would be an escape route, a door with an exit sign. One Sunday afternoon in August, I clipped an announcement from the *Toronto Telegram*, figured out the mysteries of the subway system and found my way to a convention hall downtown. There I scrutinized exhibits about how to keep food for long periods of time, and took notes on staying warm underground during a Canadian nuclear winter.

After graduating from university, I took the train west to the coast. I had job leads in Edmonton and Vancouver, so I researched each city's escape plan. Every municipality, now as well as then, has a strategy in the event of disaster. Edmonton felt safer; there were highways out of town. Vancouver made me nervous – all those mountains hemming you in on one side, the unforgiving ocean on the other. During a beautiful summer on Wreck Beach, while my new friends were falling in and out of love, I read survival manuals and discovered that the most organized city in North America was Seattle. They had a clear chain of command, one person to make a decision and put the action plan into effect: the fire chief. I considered moving there.

I spent that distant summer under ancient Pacific cedars, stripping off my clothes and listening to arguments about the coup in Chile, capitalism and the price of bombs. It was glamorous and free. The mountains were beautiful and it was, after all, the edge of the world. I closed my eyes under an August sun and dreamed of friendships that offered a new kind of power. My parents were kilometres away, lost in show business and frivolity and alcohol. I was twenty-one and ready to stake a claim. I crossed an ocean for the first time and spent a week in London with a vivacious Winnipeg Mennonite named Gillian, who had fled her strict religious upbringing for the mysteries of Europe. I adored camping out in her freezing flat near King's Cross Station and savoured the assorted friends who arrived at all hours. Gill and I wandered the streets and consumed endless cups of murky tea.

I understand now that I stayed with Gillian – a friend of a friend – because I didn't have the courage to strike out on my own. I'd spent my first days in London at a hostel with three high-school pals. All of us were away from home for the first time and began our first night on the town over pints and chips at a pub. I enjoyed meeting the friendly crowd at the bar, but when a young couple invited us to a private party, I went on red alert. *Who are these people? Do they want something from us?* Suspicion and distrust were my default responses in those days. I fidgeted nervously while my friends agreed to join the couple across town.

The pimply boy in bell-bottoms scribbled an address on the back of a napkin. My friends downed their beers and we elbowed our way out of the crowded pub. Dana, our bossy, fearless leader, waved down a black cab and shoved the address at the driver. As we navigated the humid summer night, I gripped my arms across my chest and memorized streets. I would stay sober so that, if there was trouble, I could lead us back to our hostel. I have no memory of the party, only anxiety and the resentful need to protect my too-trusting friends. I said goodbye to them two days later, gathered my courage and telephoned Gill.

The two of us hit it off immediately, and Gillian didn't hesitate to share her amazement at the bravado of North American women. It was something she had noticed after moving to England. "Honestly, we are always talking about the future!" Gill rested her chin in her hands and frowned. "We think anything is possible. These Brits are all cluttered with their past. They've got history under every rock!" Was I a typical North American?

When William Faulkner won the Nobel Prize in Literature in 1949, he spoke about the curse of not having a future: "There are no longer problems of the spirit," he said. "There is only the question: When will I be blown up?" In *Hiroshima in America: Fifty Years of Denial*, Robert Jay Lifton and Greg Mitchell write that since 1945, personal losses – the death of a loved one, dislocation from home – have merged with extreme threat. "Just as, after Hiroshima, every antagonism between nations takes on the potential for destroying the entire world, so does every personal trauma potentially take on that end-of-the-world association."[2] Every danger we experience, public or private, puts us psychically on the edge of disaster, worrying about the next emergency: an earthquake in Japan, an oil spill in the Gulf, a friend with cancer, an alcoholic parent.

For North Americans, the September 11 attacks didn't create the visceral, urgent sense of threat to home and security; they merely ripped off the protective scab that had grown over the wounds of 1945. We still live in fear – of terrorism, of radiation contamination, of the apocalypse. The twentysomething man who owns the corner store near my house says he doesn't think about nuclear weapons. But he knows the planet will have no edible food in ten years, so he keeps tins and seed packets in the basement. This is what humans do when faced with danger: we hide, conceal ourselves; we seek shelter. Like Adam, we are always running for cover. God asks Adam, "Where are you?" Goethe replies, "If I knew myself, I'd run away."

While working on this book I met a stranger at a party who asked what I was doing. "Trying to connect my childhood to my obsession with disaster and war," I said. Her face lit up. "I know all about that! When the accident happened at Three Mile Island, I was scared shitless." In 1979, this stranger, Anna, had lived just a few hundred kilometres from the Pennsylvania nuclear power plant. For days after the accident she stockpiled food and water in the basement and repeated to her husband, "We'll be okay." Anna's husband had lived in South Africa until he was twenty-one. He knew what a constant state of emergency could do to people. "Be 'okay'? That isn't life; that's just survival," he had told her. "You have to live to make the world *more* than that." So the couple decided to have a baby. They needed a reason to work for a better world. They needed to get Anna out of the basement.

Physics historian Spencer Weart studies nuclear fear. When people are traumatized by something they can't see or feel, they never really know whether they have been harmed. He writes that their "uncertainty never ends: they feel they have been damaged for life." The result, particularly when governments and authorities withhold explanations, is an absence of trust in human institutions and the natural world. This is the psychic damage that Faulkner was talking about, and it's what was wrong with the newspaper article I read that morning in my apartment. How can uncertainty be ironed out? How do we "move on" from what happened when the sky exploded over Hiroshima when the impact of nuclear fear has never even been registered as real?

The difficulty of measuring nuclear threat makes it invisible and terrifying at the same time. We become afraid of contamination by association. In Goiânia, Brazil, in 1987, two men salvaging scrap metal accidentally released radioactive materials from an abandoned cancer therapy device. Four people died and several hundred were contaminated. If this had been a non-nuclear chemical accident, the matter would have ended there. But because it was nuclear, the entire Goiânia region was stigmatized. According to Weart, "Hotels in other parts of the country refused to allow Goiânia residents to register, airline pilots refused to fly with Goiânia residents on board, automobiles driven by Goiânians were stoned."[3] In 2011, this will happen to people living on the northeast coast of Japan. After the accident at Fukushima, neighbours will be afraid to let their daughters and sons play with children who lived closer to the power plant. Grandparents will have to travel to Tokyo to visit their relocated grandchildren because nobody knows how far away from the accident is far enough. On the western coast of

North America, families will warn each other that objects washed up on the beach might be dangerous.

I am not old enough to remember the *Duck and Cover* film and others like it, but part of my research getting ready for this trip involves screening them at my university library. The cartoons were designed in the '50s to teach children how to survive a nuclear war. What strikes me while watching is how easy it is to laugh at their naïveté: the father putting a newspaper over his head; the wrinkled turtle with the wise, ancient voice giving advice. Most chilling is the clarity of the message: a nuclear attack will come without warning and there will be NO adults to help you.

In each cartoon, little children do ordinary things. Tony rides his tricycle down the block and FLASH! he falls and huddles by the curb. Paul and Patty, brother and sister, walk out of a suburban house and FLASH! they dive against a building. Be vigilant at all times for it can happen day or night, at school, anywhere. You have to be ready. Never let down your guard.

My friend Barbara was born in 1970, well after the height of the Cold War. When she turned nine she realized it was necessary to have a plan for nuclear war. Barbara lived in a small village in Nova Scotia, so she chose a neighbouring city where she and her family could join a large group of people to help one another. Being away from her family at Girl Guide camp gave Barbara early morning panic attacks. "It wasn't that I wanted to be home, it was just that it was not easy to organize *all* the Girl Guides in case of nuclear war. Later, when I became interested in boys, it became more of a death fantasy. Which of my friends or crushes did I want to die with?"

I'm older than Barbara – I was born in 1955 – but I don't remember being influenced by Cold War propaganda. I don't think we had drills at my school to prepare us for nuclear explosions. But culture is something you breathe in. It's invisible. It doesn't matter if we remember it consciously or not. One day, while walking home after watching duck and cover cartoons in the library, some-thing flashed in my head – an incident I'd completely forgotten but had such an impact on me that recalling it made me dizzy. Something I witnessed by accident in 1966 that gave everything that frightened me inside my home an external source. It married the threat of the world outside to the psychological war zone I hid from every day.

It started with my favourite babysitter. I can't remember her name, but she was Swedish and carried a floppy tie-dyed bag that held treasures presented only after our parents had left for the evening. My brother grabbed his Dinky car and disappeared. I was overcome with gratitude as my tall, Nordic heroine pulled out two packages bound in frayed ribbon and tissue paper. Each parcel contained a tiny knitted outfit for my Barbie doll. I remem-ber silky grey cardigans, flashy red skirts and an orange floppy hat with matching long-sleeved gloves. My Barbie looked like nothing found on the Paris runways that summer of '66, but I paraded her with pride up and down the hallway of our third-floor Victorian attic.

My Barbie had ash-blonde hair to her shoulders and perfect square bangs. I loved the power I had to dress her, to choose what covered her cold plastic. I bent her legs and stared longingly at her curved breasts and hips. She was too sharp to hug, but I wanted to be strong like I imagined her to be. Barbie and her wardrobe were my only comfort. Sleeping alone on the top floor, exposed to the street where anyone passing could look up and see in my tiny window, terrified me.

My brother and I each had a small attic bedroom, mine at the front and his at the back of a large house we could afford because mother had a role in a Canadian soap opera. This year of living bountifully – we moved twelve months later when the show was cancelled – included many nights out for my parents. Perhaps it was simply being so far from the adults that frightened me, or the feeling that I had to protect my younger brother who slept un-disturbed at the other end of Barbie's runway. Or perhaps it was because that was the summer Richard Speck murdered all those nurses.

We watched updates on the killings, my brother, the babysit-ter and I, in front of our black-and-white television in the living room. They kept showing a diagram of the victims' house, with numbers and dotted lines that traced the trajectory of the man and the place where each woman was killed. Speck had knocked on the door of a Chicago townhouse occupied by student nurses. He tied up six of them and waited for three more to return home from their dates, and then systematically stabbed, raped and strangled all but one who'd huddled far enough in a dark corner under a bed to escape detection. Speck was high on drugs and alcohol, franti-cally aroused, and had lost count. This small detail saved Corazon Amurao's life.

That was in early July. The women were found the morning of July 14, but Speck wasn't arrested until several days later. He had attempted suicide and then turned himself in at a local hospital. Someone on staff recognized the tattoo on his arm; it said "Born to Raise Hell." I think of him sitting there, in that hospital. With the nurses.

The babysitter and I were glued to the news. I drank in every detail of this secret we shared. I have no recollection of saying anything to my parents. If it happened today, I'm sure somebody would have forbidden us to watch. Those were different times; television was new enough that its presence in the house was a charming distraction, hardly something pointing to the reality be-yond the screen. But I absorbed what was happening as if it were my street, each woman someone I knew intimately, but couldn't protect. I can't help thinking, do children respond this way today? Drinking in images of death through their cell phones?

Now, brought back to this incident by the duck and cover films and my immersion in atomic trauma, I google Speck to learn details beyond what I remember. This is the first time in almost forty years I have looked at this name, this photograph, these details. As I read, I recognize and even remember the women's names.

A friend of mine thinks there was a *Life* magazine article about the murders, so I look it up and order it from Amazon. The thirty-five-cent July 29, 1966, issue arrives by FedEx in tight cardboard wrapping and I push it behind some books in my study. It's a month before I have the nerve to open it. The feature article is by Loudon Wainwright, father of Loudon Wainwright III and grandfather to Rufus. It is called, simply, "The Nine Nurses."[4]

On the cover is a photograph of Speck's fingerprint on the door to the women's residence. It is 1966; the year Martin Luther King, Jr., brought the Civil Rights Movement north to Chicago. Inside the magazine, Mia Farrow has just married Frank Sinatra. To be a nurse, and to live away from home, is part of a new world for young women – the excitement of independence, opportunity. It is one year before the Summer of Love, that last vibrant gasp of the '60s.

Wainwright took the time to find out small details in the lives of each of the students in the house that night, details that got "buried in the litter of such an appalling crime."[5] Merlita Gargullo, Valentina Pasion and Corazon Amurao were registered nurses from the Philippines who came to America via an international exchange program. Valentina was a wonderful cook, and Merlita loved to swim in the river near her village. Mary Ann Jordan, one of the five Americans, lived with her parents and was visiting her friends overnight. Gloria Davy was elegant and often asked her roommates to get her out of bed in the mornings. Pam Wilkening's nickname was Willie, Pat Matusek was proud of her thick and lustrous hair, and Nina Schmale made everyone laugh.

It was a year of new possibilities and freedoms. Betty Friedan founded the National Organization for Women with a mandate to make women full partners with men. Merlita was the first person from her village to go to America. Pam was saving for a car of her own and Gloria wanted to join the Peace Corps. As Wainwright told it, Cora Amurao, four feet ten inches tall, didn't believe the man who said he only wanted money to get to New Orleans. She'd seen a gun and a thin-bladed knife.

The man, dressed in black, ripped up bedsheets, blindfolded and tied the women, then led one of them out of the bedroom and closed the door. Cora, able to loosen her hands, whispered frantically to the others that they could free themselves, hit the man with a steel bunk ladder, leap on him and overpower him. For whatever reason, writes Wainright, "the others told her to keep still. In despair because she could not get them to act, Corazon Amurao then rolled under one of the beds and hid."[6]

In 1966, I became obsessed with Corazon Amurao. I needed to know how to do what she had done. For the rest of that summer, and into the fall and winter, I sat in my bedroom window keeping watch. I waited for the man who would come along the street, turn into our yard, enter our house. While my brother and parents slept, I kept watch.

I bury the *Life* magazine at the bottom of a box. But I keep thinking about it. When I'm supposed to be working, I find myself at the computer, trolling for more details about that day in Chicago. I check the weather; summers there can be brutal. It was Bastille Day. I suppose in France they were celebrating. I wonder about Corazon. I know her mother flew from their village of Durango, sixty-eight kilometres south of Manila, to be with her daughter. Did they both return home to the Philippines? What does Cora see when she closes her eyes? I think perhaps I should google her, but it seems a violation. I find a sensationalist article from a Chicago paper, "Forty Years Later!" the headline screams. The top of the long column says that the lone survivor of the murders declined requests for an interview. Good for you, I think, and close the computer.

It is years before I understand what this memory has to do with my preoccupation with atomic threat. To try and make sense of it, I turn first to science, and then to story. I read about western medicine, the brain and trauma. I look east, toward Japan, and what it means to be haunted.

Western science tells me that experiences that set off a chain reaction of anxiety and distrust are easily triggered by encounters in our lives, some of them as innocent as a night at the movies. Primary emotions impact us at the chemical level. Strong experiences – assault, abandonment, accident – take up residence in our bodies. The response to a core emotion is both cognitive – we think something has happened – and felt. Because of how our brains work, the strong experience can be unleashed by situations that remind us of the original encounter. When I watch a face slapped on a movie screen, neurons in my brain act as if my own face is being slapped. The movie has the power to return us to the original moment of terror. This is the physiology behind post-traumatic stress disorder.

In the cultural imagination of Japan, there is a vital connection between the living and the dead. An extensive network of rituals and ceremonies plays an important role in assisting the passage to the underworld and honouring those who have died. According to the history of the village of Kamimachi, a wealthy family once controlled the surrounding harsh and mountainous Toyama region.

In the nineteenth century, peasants rose up and killed them all: men, women and children. Today, the community holds an annual festival to "call back" the life forces of those murdered. "Without the proper execution of rites for the dead, spirits cannot rest, and become, as a result, these hungry, wandering spirits called muen-botoke (buddhas without attachment or affiliation) or gaki (hungry ghosts),"[7] who present a dangerous threat to the living. Failure to meet this obligation is said to result in haunting. The spirits of murder victims and children are particularly dangerous.[8]

I am trying to remember the spots that I have been drawn to in my life, and the ghosts that have summoned me. These are haunted places, laden with memory. Burial sites: bits of bone, a cough behind a tree, a whisper on the air. Shadows, stories, headlines, names scratched into the flint of old gravestones. The act of mourning is a ritual of digging.

THREE

It's a dream, but I don't know if I'm awake or asleep. There are two of them, a man and a woman, stumbling along this apparently deserted highway. The man carries a heavy knapsack of books. He takes a few steps, stops, looks up and sniffs the air. It's dry, so cold the ice snaps. The man types into a small laptop computer. He checks the GPS and mutters to himself. The woman looks worried. She has no books, no computer, no point of reference. She carries a blue nylon bag stuffed with warm socks, extra shoes, a shopping list and a bundle of airline tickets. They are very far from home and this is deliberate. They are already uncomfortable and inadequately dressed. Travel is a risky venture. Neither has a passport. Neither has a compass. All they know is, they're headed north.

To begin their journey, they have to learn a little something about radiation. The device they use for measuring levels is called a Geiger counter. If you flick it on in Kiev, Ukraine, for example, it measures twelve to sixteen microroentgen per hour or more. One roentgen is one hundred thousand times the average radiation of a typical city. A dose of five hundred roentgens within five hours is fatal to humans. It takes about two and a half times that dosage to kill a chicken and over one hundred times that to kill a cockroach.

The woman wishes she had brought dark glasses; the sun's glare off the ice hurts her eyes. So does reading her companion's computer screen. They don't know much. They know that at the mine site on the eastern shore of Great Bear Lake, hand-processed uranium ore was bagged into ninety-pound sacks, loaded onto barges and moved over 2,300 kilometres of lake, river and portage to the railhead at Waterways, Alberta. They know that the route they are following touches the Aboriginal labourers employed to transport the ore, the white miners who worked underground, the employees of Eldorado that ran the mine site and the men who worked for the Northern Transportation Company, running riverboats and flying materials in and out of Port Radium. It extends to a uranium refinery in Port Hope, Ontario; into America and the desert of New Mexico; and, finally, to Japan.

What are the proper instruments for exploring the highway of the atom? A Geiger counter, a shotgun, a tape recorder, a pair of socks?

The man makes a note: the northern traveller always tends to over-pack.

I have this dream repeatedly during the months that Peter and I spend preparing to go to Déline. We haven't yet gotten our grant from the Canadian government and we want to be ready. I scramble to learn all I can about Great Bear Lake, the Eldorado Mine and atomic history. I've put my personal crisis on hold, but it returns in the dream. Who, I wonder, is my guide? And what kind of inferno are we heading into?

Peter sends me *When the World was New*, a book by George Blondin. Blondin was in his seventies when he went with the Dene delegation to Hiroshima. He was the first to write down the story that many in Déline tell to visitors. The community is hard at work collecting documentation that testifies to their relationship to uranium mining and Déline's history. But this story, told in different ways, is the community's account of Eldorado and all that came after the "discovery" of the mine. Because Blondin published in English, it has been shared with the outside world.

Long ago there was a famous rock called *Somba Ké*, known as "the money place." Loud noises came from this place and it was bad medicine to pass near it. In the old days, a group of caribou hunters camped there. One of them, a man named Louis Ayah, dreamed he saw many strange things. "The medicine man told them of his strange vision. 'I saw people going into a big hole in the ground – strange people, not Dene. Their skin was white...On the surface where they lived, there were strange houses with smoke coming out of them... [I saw] big boats with smoke... I saw a flying bird – a big one. They were loading it with things... I watched them . . . I wanted to know what it was for – I saw what harm it would do when the big bird dropped this thing on people.'"[9]

This would happen sometime in the future, after we are all gone, the prophet said. In his vision everyone died. Everyone burned.

Déline is an indigenous community of several hundred people in the Northwest Territories. In the 1930s and '40s, the people of Déline ferried hand-processed bags of uranium ore from the Eldorado Mine – where Somba Ké was first pointed out – across Great Bear Lake. The sacs were carried on men's backs, loaded onto boats and transported about two thousand kilometres south to Alberta, where they then travelled by rail to the refinery in Port Hope, in southern Ontario. The processed uranium ore was sent to the Manhattan Project in New Mexico, where it contributed to developing the atomic bomb dropped on Hiroshima.

For decades the *Sahtúgot'ine* Bear Lake People had heard ru-
mours about where the uranium mined from their land ended up.
In the 1990s, a meeting in Toronto between the Dene and Gor-
don Edwards, co-founder of the Canadian Coalition for Nuclear
Responsibility, confirmed the deadly tie binding Port Radium to
Hiroshima.

Then, fifty-seven years after Hiroshima was bombed, a delegation
of Sahtú Dene from Déline travelled to Japan to make an apology.
Their trip was the result of a long and careful process; they talked,
listened, consulted. The elders were with them. This was not an
individual act; they went to send their respects. They went because
the beginning was meeting the end.

It is this apology that Peter and I keep returning to in our conversations. We write endless emails back and forth but can't get
our heads around it. How was the decision made? Was it obvious?
Was it challenged by anyone? Is this a question we can even ask?
What this raises, for us, are questions of responsibility, relationship and custody. When is it a privilege to be the guardians of a
place, a community and a story, and when does it become a form
of imprisonment? Do some people in Déline just want the whole
narrative concerning the mine to go away? What kind of debt do
any of us have to the past? Is the Dene's radical connection to the
land and their willingness to accept responsibility on its behalf a
debt they are obliged to pay, or a gift they are blessed with offering?

Exhausted by our own questions, we turn to available information. The most detailed and plain-speaking document is *They
Never Told Us These Things*, a report about Eldorado the Dene researched, wrote and carried to Ottawa in 1998. We read that, from
the beginning of the mine's operations, the government had kept
crucial information from the Dene. In 1932, the *Annual Report of
the Department of Mines* mandated weekly lung tests for radium
miners, as well as monthly blood tests for lab workers – but only

in Canada's south. The 1933 report included a lengthy and detailed examination of the ore's dangers: "when the insidious and deadly nature of radium is considered, too much care cannot be taken."[10] But nobody told the Dene who carried and transported it. Nor, it seems, did anyone tell the white miners who worked underground, and who also lived at Port Radium.

Cindy Kenny-Gilday, a Dene activist and a major force behind the trip to Hiroshima, writes about a packed community meeting in Déline where lawyers delivered a year's worth of uranium-impact research from the national archives. "'In the mountain of papers we dug up in Ottawa this year on this issue, there is not one mention of the Dene, your people,'" the lawyers say in Kenny-Gilday's retelling. "The hall went completely silent. The elders had incredulous looks on their faces, a combination of sadness and anger."[11]

Next, I watch *Village of Widows*, Canadian filmmaker Peter Blow's 1999 documentary. I sit on my couch, my cat in my lap, and consider the flickering images, my first introduction to these people that I will someday meet. Blow visited the community and accompanied the ten Dene to Japan. George Blondin is interviewed. The film uses historical footage to tell the story of Eldorado in its heyday. Blow also met with white workers who now live in Edmonton, including Derek Likert, who was the son of a supervisor at Eldorado. Likert talks on camera about a sandbox built on the mine site for kids to play in at recess. There was no sand so they used mine tailings. He describes the stuff as pulverized and ground out of the ball mill: it "just blows around like a bag of flour if you left it in the wind."

The Dene delegation didn't only meet with the Japanese; they also visited a hospital in the back streets of Hiroshima devoted to the approximately thirty thousand Korean forced labourers working

in the city in 1945. Peter Blow was with them, filming. As I watch
the film in 2002 it is an old Dene man's testimony to the Korean
patients that stops me. I rewind the tape four or five times to make
sure I heard him correctly. I write down what he's saying, and put
numbers beside each phrase so that the order is right.

1. with my dog team I helped load that plane
2. uranium, pure uranium on that plane
3. where they convert it to atomic bombs and drop it here
4. I worked one day, and I often thought about that
5. I never thought, I never thought
6. you don't know nothing
7. I thought it was gold. I thought they made rings, or something
   in the south

I'm slowly preparing for the trip, and my personal life has
perked up. I'm seeing a nice guy, he makes me laugh. Maybe I can
handle this intense work after all. Even asking "Who am I to com-
plain?" feels indulgent. I have a job, good friends, a bit of romance
and a purpose. Life may not be beautiful, but it's good.

In January of 2003, Peter and I receive an email from Déline. It
is good timing for the community if we come the following month.
We aren't ready; we hadn't planned to make the trip for another six
months, but the Band Council has invited us. We start packing.

There's a flurry of activity as we arrange tickets and finalize
plans, and I find myself in a panic. I stop sleeping and scribble
endlessly in notebooks. I want to remember this awkwardness,
this paralysis, this clumsy approach – what it means to know that
I know nothing. What had we said in our grant proposal, something about stumbling down the highway of the atom as bewildered strangers searching for an ethical art of memory? It sounded
good on paper.

I calm myself by thinking through what I have been writing about for years: how to approach a story I don't understand. First, to be a witness is to allow myself to be opened beyond myself, to be surprised: to listen for the evidence, the facts, and to hear what exists beyond language. This is particularly true with trauma, which asks us to witness the incomprehensible. Next, I must find the resources to respond. It isn't only passing on a story that matters; I have to let the story change me. That's where the bearing of witness – the carrying of the event – comes in. By listening with openness and being changed I make myself vulnerable in the face of another's vulnerability. I participate in a relationship.

It is several years before I realize that I thought about only one thing as I prepared to go to Déline: trauma, cancer and uranium. It didn't occur to me – yet – that there was more to be seen and sensed. In my anxiety about visiting an unfamiliar community I was looking, I think, for the authority to enter the world of the people of Déline. This would only be possible if I could figure out what in my own life was taking me there. I didn't know it at the time, but this was also on Peter's mind. When he eventually publishes his book *The Highway of the Atom* it will include these words from Kevin Dwyer: "In order to pursue the other, one must become able to pursue the self; and the self must therefore be exposed. Anthropologists, perhaps sensing that to expose the self is necessarily to place it in jeopardy, have for the most part been unwilling to take such a gamble . . . They have refused to admit that the very possibility of dealing . . . with the other is tied to the capacity to put the self at stake."[12]

As Peter and I exchange email lists of what to pack, I am reminded of a project I worked on as a graduate student. It strikes me as a cautionary tale for the trip I am about to make. I was an assistant to my supervisor, Roger Simon, and his team of researchers. The job was to figure out what was involved in teaching and passing on stories of the forced migration of Inuit in the Eastern Canadian Arctic. One day, at a meeting I did not attend, my colleagues met with a woman from the Inuit community. She expressed concern: Why were these white southerners involving themselves in her people's stories? Our research group had no response except to quickly withdraw from the project. When I heard what had happened I was disturbed. I was too shy to speak up but wanted to ask, "Why was this decision made so fast? What if others in that Inuit community had felt differently? Why did one judgment carry such weight? As white scholars, what does it mean if we immediately apologize and withdraw?"

Trying to make sense of my own self-absorption, I dig through files and find an essay by philosophy professor Deanne Bogdan. When the World Trade Center was attacked on 9/11, Deanne was about to teach a seminar at the University of Toronto. She wondered how to acknowledge what had just happened and decided to play a piece of music as a memorial to the victims. She agonized over what to pick. Deanne hadn't met any of the students. Where were they from? What were their religious and cultural backgrounds? What were their experiences with violence? She decided to play something she herself loved, Fauré's Requiem, but then hesitated. After all, she had selected a Catholic mass for the dead. What kind of message might that send? After eliminating several other options, she got so worried about offending someone that she played nothing.

Bogdan confesses in the article to a failure of nerve. Though I understand how she made her decision, I think it's crazy. I know Deanne. She is a smart, compassionate woman and an accomplished musician who recognizes the power and importance of music. She made a thoughtful choice when she came up with Requiem. Then she panicked. It wasn't the music that Deanne didn't trust; it was herself. This is the kind of paralysis I'm feeling about this trip. Do I have a right to visit people I know so little about? Will I offend people with my ignorance of their history? I put down the essay in exasperation, at Deanne and at myself. This isn't useful reflection; it's narcissism and of no help to anyone.

Kenyan writer Ngũgĩ wa Thiong'o describes meeting activists and solidarity workers who have characteristics in common: an indeterminate economic position and a lack of identity. They don't know how to define themselves as a class and they don't feel connected to a community. To fill this gap they seek belonging in the struggles of others. He blames this "vacillating psychological makeup"[13] on how colonialism controls "not only political and economic wealth, but the entire realm of the language of real life."[14] I recognize myself in Wa Thiong'o's description. I am reminded of a quote from my activist days, credited to Lily Watson, an Aboriginal woman in Australia: "If you have come here to help me you are wasting our time. If you have come because your liberation is bound up with mine, then let's work together."

Taking up Watson's challenge, I turn to the shadows in my own history.

FOUR

My high school auditorium is packed with smelly adolescents. The chairs are rickety and old and snag my pantyhose. The lights go halfway down – there are no blinds, the sunlight comes in when they show a movie – and the chubby, frowning principal tells us to be prepared because we are going to see mature content. I am pleased to be mature and decide to remember everything.

The movie is about Scotland, the clans and a man called Bonnie Prince Charlie. It's thrilling and dramatic – they want to seize their country back from the powerful English who have starved and brutalized them. This prince is going to lead the honest and hard-working men to victory. The clans wear kilts and have their own crests and patterns; one might be Scott, which is my mother's name. Her father, my grandfather, Bert Scott, lives with us and sings funny songs that come from this part of my background. I'm riveted to the screen. I didn't know my ancestors experienced this terrible oppression. It's the night before the big battle.

The clansmen are tired and hungry, but Charlie tells them to keep fighting. One more day.

Then it isn't such a nice movie anymore. The screen fills with blood, swords cutting off arms and horses screaming. I stare at the floor and grind my hands into my seat. I find a crack in the wood and it hurts and I push harder, my hand bleeds, I want the thing to be over. The lights come up. I push fast out to the washroom and don't ask permission. I slam the door and sit in the stall and cry over this brutal, idiotic betrayal. A prince is supposed to know what he's doing.

Fifteen years later, I'm travelling by train through Scotland and find myself in Inverness near dark. The Highland city used to be a fort; it's Saturday night, and there are drunken kids on the streets. I head to the river. Despite the wet weather it is beautiful, illuminated by lanterns. I find a small hotel and the owner offers me a cheese sandwich. In the lobby is a counter with brochures. I read one while drinking a cup of strong tea. It mentions a tour to a local woollen mill, a stop at Loch Ness – there's a glossy picture of the monster rising from the lake – and the Culloden Battlefield. I stuff the flyer in my pocket, flushed with an excitement I don't understand. I unpack, but it's too early to sleep, so I find a bench by the river and sit until midnight.

I'm part Scottish and I'm trying to figure out what that means. In my experience, the British Isles are mixed together in a sameness called "white Anglo-Saxon," which means privileged westerner. I'm aware that there were clearances and famine in this country, but it's never occurred to me that I could make a claim on this history and that what happened to my great-grandparents could impact their descendant. I imagine writing a letter home to ask about my grandfather on my mother's side. "Dear Mum. Did Bampa ever go to Scotland? Why did we only hear Dad's Icelandic stories? Were you angry your Irish-Scottish-English background was written off as bland and boring? Were your Scottish ancestors farmers? They couldn't have been landowners or we'd have had money. When did they come to Canada?"

The morning is crisp and cloudy. I board a white bus with "Highland Adventures" painted on the front. We drive into the countryside, stopping briefly at the mill, and then follow the shoreline of the famous sullen lake. The guide is a wrinkled stick of a man. He tells a story about the famous monster and finally the bus turns into an empty parking lot. We step down onto the edge of the Culloden Battlefield.

We have one hour. I escape the group and stride across dark, uneven fields. There are groves of stumpy trees, bits of rock poking through the grass, mist everywhere. I think of *Wuthering Heights* but that feels blasphemous. There's nothing English about this place; this is where some of my people came from and it was the English who murdered them. I can hardly breathe. I remember the documentary I'd seen as a teenager, where Bonnie Prince Charlie led exhausted Highlanders to be slaughtered by the British. It was the last hand-to-hand combat in Britain. It was brutal and bloody. The young, arrogant prince caused the deaths of hundreds that day.

I step out of my Birkenstocks, muddy from last night's wild rain, and force my eyes shut. I want to feel this place. At first I'm self-conscious – stupid tourist – but I push away the voice in my head and concentrate. I remember seeing a play called *Jessica*, written through collaboration between Métis playwright Maria Campbell and Linda Griffiths, an actor of Scottish heritage. Although the subject of the play was Campbell's life, Campbell was impatient with how Griffiths was in such awe regarding the tragedy of Aboriginal history and kept saying, "I'm ashamed that I didn't know." Campbell tells Griffiths, "While you were being overwhelmed by my oppression, you were making me feel it was exclusively mine.

I couldn't understand why you didn't know your own history, the clearances but also the magic and power of it, how so many were burned as witches, tortured. Then I could have said to you, 'this is what happened to my grandfathers,' and you could have said, 'this is what happened to mine.'"[15]

I take a step and almost trip on a small headstone. They're everywhere, crudely marked with the names of the clans. I get down on my knees and put both hands on the dark, wet slab. The writing is illegible. I look across the meadow. There are tiny white flowers everywhere.

Our tour group has gathered by the bus. I tell the guide I want to stay longer. He frowns. "My afternoon bus doesn't stop at Culloden."

"I'll be fine," I say. "I'll call a cab." Reluctantly, he gives in. I watch with relief as the bus plods down the lane and turns out of sight.

I spend an hour inside the visitor's museum and am then compelled to return to the empty meadow. I walk all afternoon, stopping by a stone cairn, a tall tree. This place feels marked by grief. I laugh at myself; I am young and have a lively imagination. The clouds break apart, the sun appears and the sky explodes with light. I smell sweet, cold air.

To my surprise, the bus returns at four that afternoon. The guide finds me reading on the cobbled patio adjoining the coffee shop. His hair is only partly white; maybe he isn't so old after all. "I've come to fetch you, young lady!" He confesses he took a detour, to the surprise of his passengers. He folds his arms and fixes me with a look.

"I have a question." I shrug and he leans forward. "What interested you about this place? I mean, the ladies, they have their particulars. It's usually the woollen mill, most of the time that's what the ladies want. Or shopping. I've never had a girl want to spend time on a battlefield!"

A few days later, I visit a bookstore in Glasgow but don't have the nerve to admit I'm interested in my ancestors. Back at my hostel, Werner, a German student joins me for a beer. He says that nobody in his country wants to think about what their parents did during the war. There is a phrase in his language for what it means to be German and young: *ein leeres bild* – an empty picture. He asks if I have something like this, a word or phrase that means Canadian. I don't.

I look back now at my young self, holding an empty picture, wondering what I was and wasn't allowed to draw inside it. I wonder if the paralysis that grips me, this anxiety about entering the Dene's atomic story, comes not from fear of *doing* the wrong thing, not even from fear of *being* the wrong thing (too white, too "from the South," too ignorant), but the absence of *being* at all.

Rosemary Jolly, a white South African writing about her work on rape and violence against women in Soweto, says that women refused to meet her in person until she explained why she was interested in their lives. "This statement did not take the form of telling them why their stories were important to the oral historical record," because "they knew that, and had had enough of white people coming into Soweto and getting information from them without giving anything back."[16] Jolly wrote them a story of her own life, forcing herself not to leave out incidents she feared they would think were trivial. The women used her story "to judge whether they would enter into a relationship with me or not. They responded sympathetically to parts of my narrative, parts that they saw as a somewhat difficult life, and I was amazed, for I had never thought I had the right to see my life in that way. In other words, they were quite willing to grant me the subject status that had eluded them, almost all their lives."[17]

Rosemary was not a paralyzed witness but a foolish one. She risked making a fool of herself, saying the wrong thing, exposing herself to ridicule, and – perhaps most importantly – she risked damaging the relationship she was building with these women. She filled in a picture of who she is and offered it. It was this vulnerability that allowed the women to approach her.

All of these writers – Rosemary Jolly, Ngũgĩ wa Thiong'o, Deanne Bogdan, Lily Watson and Maria Campbell – are telling me something. "Draw it now," I hear them say. "Don't try so hard to figure it out. Sit down with us and tell us who you are. Tell us why you are coming."

FIVE

A place of spiritual beauty, silence, even transcendence, and of terror
– a place of isolation, madness and death. To the Southern mind,
the North is a paradox: it is at once empty – with nothing but lakes,
rivers, forests, muskeg, taiga, tundra and ice – and full – full of exotic
peoples, caribou, mineral riches, unsolved mysteries, and ghosts.
– Sherrill Grace, Introduction, Staging North: Twelve Canadian Plays

Great Bear Lake is more than three hundred square kilometres of
inland sea, close to the treeline. It is bordered on the south and
west by black and white spruce, with a sprinkling of muskeg; on
its northern edge, the forest gives way to tundra. This is the land
of the Sahtúgot'ine. During the 1930s, a village sprang up around
the site of the Eldorado Mine on the lake's eastern shore. There was
a school, a store and lodging for the white miners. Yukon Jess, a
madam who had seen fortunes made and lost in the Klondike, ran
a brothel until both her girls ran off with the customers. One year,
the circus came to town.

Gilbert LaBine, an Ottawa Valley boy, arrived at Great Bear
in 1929. Hiring a plane wasn't cheap, but the odds were high that
this experienced miner would find silver or copper. He was forty
years old and the co-owner of Eldorado Gold Mines. LaBine was
flown in by Canadian Airway's veteran Leigh Britnell. He was later
picked up and flown out by the legendary "Punch" Dickens, a former fighter pilot decorated for service in France and famous for

adventurous flights into the bush. Dickens had purchased a new American aircraft called the Fokker Super Universal. This tough little plane had a new feature everyone was talking about: an enclosed cockpit. It was also adaptable, with wheels, floats and skis, and could land on water or snow. The model was so perfect for cold weather that explorer Richard E. Byrd chose it for his 1928 flight to the Antarctic.

Maybe it's the story of my mother and her first husband, the pilot and young lover I can only imagine, but I am fascinated by early pilots in the north. In an interview with historian George Inglis, Dickens describes flying LaBine down the coast of Great Bear on a sunny afternoon. The small plane coasted over rugged countryside bordered by the sharp rise of 400-foot cliffs. As he swung over Echo Bay on the eastern corner of the lake, Dickens felt a tap on his shoulder. He turned to see his passenger pointing down at Gossan Island, a small jewel sparkling in the blue water, a vivid mix of cobalt-bloom and copper-green.

"Can you find the place again?" LaBine asked. "I want to come back."

At the time Gilbert LaBine was flying into the sunrise over Great Bear, world demand for radium had skyrocketed. The medical benefits of external radium therapy, to stop the growth of cancerous tumours, meant that anyone who found pitchblende would do well. The dark, shimmering substance included uranium and radium. It had been known about in Europe since the early sixteenth century, but was hard to find outside of the Belgian Congo.

LaBine returned in March of 1930, accompanied by prospector Charles St. Paul. The two men were dropped at the Camsell River just east of Great Bear and made their way north toward Hunter Bay, where stakes marked a number of previous claims. St. Paul was stricken with snow blindness and confined to a tent, leaving LaBine to prospect alone. It didn't take him long to discover silver and a vein of pitchblende just across from Gossan Island, near what would become LaBine Point. Many years later, after August 6, 1945, a reporter commented: "If Charlie Saint Paul hadn't gone snowblind, Hiroshima would probably still be perpendicular."

It is February 14, 2002. Valentine's Day. Peter and I have escaped our universities and made it through airport security in Toronto. Everything changes when you fly north. From the airline magazine I tear out a glossy photo of a small tent hovering under a swirl of jade and make a note: "Remember Japanese newlyweds who camp under the aurora borealis. It's a lucky place to conceive a child." This is sweetly romantic and something my new boyfriend would love, except he doesn't want children. He doesn't want commitment either, so honeymoons under the northern lights are out. We have been together almost a year and he is tearfully in love with me when drinking and confusingly diffident when sober. In my suitcase I carry a passionate note he scribbled in pencil as I said goodbye and hopped a cab for Pearson airport. "You mean the world to me. Have fun up north."

North is a word most Canadians use with a vague sense of romance, evoking a heritage we claim with little understanding or even curiosity. We fly from western Canada to Europe, glancing down through airplane windows, thrilled to lay claim to a land not yet domesticated, alive in our imaginations for these brief hours of flight. As my plane begins its descent into Norman Wells I'm physically unsettled by this change in the pattern of my life's journeys. Today I am not in a large jet heading leisurely toward London or Paris. Today I descend abruptly.

This land looks like nothing I've ever seen. The snow goes on forever. I clutch hot coffee and fasten my seat belt as the left wing dives into a cloud. The sun shoots over my right shoulder and with a ceremonial bump we taxi along the asphalt airstrip. Peter and I have a four-hour stopover before going on to Déline. The plane door swings open and Arctic wind blasts my face. The intensity of light is disorienting; the sky is endless and powder blue, deep and dusty. I grip the railing and descend to the tarmac. I sense that no one is behind me, stop and turn around. Peter is still at the top of the steps, framed in the plane's narrow opening. As if he has all the time in the world to savour this first moment. He stoops his tall frame, ducks under the doorway and hurries down the narrow metal stairs.

I have been trying to catch up on everything I didn't learn in school, reading bits of history – the Sahtú Dene, Inuit, Dogrib, Yellowknife and Northern Cree. The Franklin expedition. All the British whose names I know and the Dene whose names I do not. "I need wisdom," writes Rudy Wiebe, "to understand why Canadians have so little comprehension of our own nordicity, that we are a northern nation." Until we grasp this imaginatively, "we will always go whoring after the mocking palm trees and beaches of the Caribbean and Florida and Hawaii; will be wishing ourselves something that we aren't, always staring south across that mockingly invisible border."[18]

Peter and I hurry through biting cold along a wide road thick with snow. To our left is a narrow band of houses and the wide expanse that is the Mackenzie River (*Deh Cho* – big river). Everywhere there are traces of the oil this place is famous for: fleets of trucks and large, round storage containers behind steel fences. Most of the Mackenzie Valley settlements were established for the fur trade, but when Alexander Mackenzie travelled the river in a twenty-five-foot canoe in 1793 he noticed something else. The Dene called the place *Le Gohlini*, "where the oil is." Over a hundred years later a group of Dene would lead geologists to the spot where Mackenzie and his entourage had seen oil seeping along the bank. I feel like an idiot for not understanding how this place got its name: Norman Wells! As we pass the Mackenzie Valley Hotel, I shout to Peter through my layers of scarves that there is supposed to be a Chinese restaurant inside. He laughs. He is already learning that food is my refuge from uncertainty.

In the 1930s, an explosion of mining activities in and around Port Radium (the site of the Eldorado Mine) and Yellowknife made Norman Wells a busy supplier for the region. There was work, lots of it, and the bustling atmosphere of the place offered a welcome respite to men and families suffering from the Great Depression that had brutalized the country. Ten years later, the US government got into the act. In the shadow of Pearl Harbor, Washington was worried that the Japanese might attack. The Americans hired whoever they could find and rushed through the winters of 1942–44 building the Canol pipeline from Norman Wells to Whitehorse, over six hundred kilometres southwest. The idea was to pipe oil all the way to Alaska. By the time the job was finished, the threat had receded and cheaper routes had been found. In 1947, the pipeline was shut off and dismantled.

Norman Wells has a small museum with a display about the Eldorado Mine. Peter and I are the only visitors. I'm wandering down an aisle of artifacts when he calls me over to look at a photograph. "Do you see what that is?" I lean closer and can make out a small bottle attached to a frame of plywood. "What?" He's grinning. "It's at Port Radium. For some reason it's sitting outside the change room, at the mine."

I lean in closer. What I'm seeing is trinitite, the olive glass-like substance made when the sand under the first atomic bomb melted and then solidified. "How could trinitite have gotten all the way from New Mexico to Great Bear Lake?" Peter shrugs. "And look, it's not even labelled trinitite." I bend and read the caption on the photo: "Alamogordo, New Mexico, July 16, 1945 – Eldorado,

Great Bear Lake, December 13, 1945 – Fused sand from the Atomic Bomb."

"Another enigma in a sea of mysteries," says Peter.

I buy a paperback in the museum gift shop: *Great Bear: A Journey Remembered*, by Frederick B. Watt, a young journalist who prospected at Great Bear in the early 1930s. The Chinese restaurant is closed so we return to the airport, munch a bag of nuts and raisins and wait for our connecting flight to Déline. I pull out Watt's book. The cover photo reminds me of my childhood camping on Georgian Bay: brooding sky, reddish cold granite and a white spray of waves rising to a scratch of scrub trees.

Watt was four years old when he arrived in Edmonton. His family worked for newspapers. Their home on Jasper Avenue was filled with visitors: flyers, cooks and prospectors telling stories of the North and, in particular, of Great Bear Lake. When the 1929 market crash brought money troubles to Watt and his new wife, he accepted an offer to fly into Great Bear before "the in-between" – the few short weeks before the winter breakup. His job was to assist prospector Eric Beck in staking new mining claims.

Watt describes being set down by bush plane fifty-five kilometres north of where the Eldorado Mine would be, in a place called Lindsley Bay. A wall of unbreachable dark precipices looms over small, offshore islands jutting above the surface of the lake. Months later, when Watt returns to life "in the Outside," he will tell his wife about the unencumbered simplicity between the two men in those early days: "Every card was face up. There was nothing that went too deep to be talked out."[19] I love this detail showing intimacy between men.

Watt and Beck make camp with help from a few other prospectors, and set out before daybreak for the long portage to Echo Bay and the area where the Eldorado Mine will be. They are looking for something I've never heard of: witness posts, the crude but legally binding claim on the land made by hungry men from cities in the South.

One of this pair was simply the lower section of a still-rooted spruce that grew at water's edge. It had been lopped off five feet above the ground and the top two feet of the stump squared by an obviously experienced axeman. On one of the white faces a carpenter's pencil had inscribed the information that would lease the claim to the staker for 12 months once his fee had been paid and registered.[20]

I show Peter this paragraph. How strange, to find the term *witness* in Watt's book attached to an actual object. Or rather, the limb of a living tree, severed and carved by a stranger who uses the stake to make a claim. And who is paid for that claim? Not the Dene, who helped them find the site in the first place.

We are an odd pair, Peter and I. A cultural geographer and a dramatist. A careful, poetic reader and a wildly diagonal thinker. It is this combination of watching and listening together that is crafting our friendship and our mutual yet separate paths along this route. We share a willingness to wait for a story's mysteries and hiding places.

The previous year, to figure out if we could survive working together on this big a project, we took a small trip. We prepared academic papers and presented them at a conference in Quebec City. Afterwards, while driving over potholed highways to Peter's home in Montreal, I asked, "Why do you want me with you on this project?" He took a long drag from the cigarette that in those years was never far from his lips and replied, "Because I imagine looking at something and wanting to know what you think."

He asks me now, while sitting in Norman Wells Airport, peering at black-and-white photos in Watt's book, "What do you make of these witness posts?" In one photo Gilbert LaBine sits on a rock, cigarette in his mouth. Beside him are his brother Charles, the pilot Punch Dickens and four other men. Dickens holds a dapper hat on his knee and wears something like a white ascot, or a scarf. There are two images of the author in the book. In one, he stands facing away from the camera, holding an axe in his right hand, long snowshoes in his left. The photograph is almost completely white; the man stands firmly on a slope of snow, left knee bent. He looks out over a canopy of winter. The line between lake and sky is barely discernible. The caption reads, "Great Bear: first view of Lindsley Bay." The other photo is of the man in profile, and says, simply, "Ted [Frederick] Watt: marooned at Conjuror Bay."[21]

"Witnessing stakes. Crazy. And where are the Dene in all this? What do you think?" Peter repeats. I'm embarrassed to tell him that I am moved by this image. It contains all the contradictions of the situation – the brutally casual act of stealing land is rendered ordinary. All a man needed was a hatchet. But the young prospector is desperate for employment. And, of course, Frederick Watt is working for someone else. He does what he is paid to do. Escaping the Depression, he works twelve hours a day assaulted by blackflies and mosquitoes, eyes swollen shut, face and hands puffed beyond recognition. The hardships are described in detail by Fred "Tiny" Peet, who worked on Great Bear in the early 1930s. Accommodations at Eldorado are a "crowded ram pasture of a place. . . . In winter frost was ever present along the walls and under the bunks, which filled every available space. . . . Everyone slept in their underwear, some with their socks on. A forty-five-gallon drum with the top cut off provided the washing and drinking water," hauled from the often frozen lake. Poker and drink kept the men's spirits up. They would urinate outside on mounds of snow. The stench was unbearable in a bunkhouse built for twelve but that housed more than thirty. Peet wrote: "If work could have been found anywhere else, I doubt if anyone would have stayed at Eldorado under these conditions."[22]

I don't share my muddled thoughts with Peter. We strike up a conversation with a young Edmonton couple that work in Déline. The woman asks if Peter is my husband and I say no. It won't be the first time this assumption is made. Years later, when Peter and I give a reading in Tokyo, a member of the audience asks if we can describe how we work together. "I think of it as 'friendship as methodology,'" says Peter. It's a good way to put it. There is no separation between these things, the thinking, the sharing and the being together on the ground.

The loudspeaker announces our flight. We gather our bags and join the others climbing into the twin propeller aircraft. I try to guess each passenger's business. The two pilots are young enough to be my students. The short, stocky one sorts through the mailbag while the spectacled kid starts the engines. A stout Dene woman with large black glasses shouts to the pilots over the roaring engine that she is back from a medical appointment in Edmonton.

Our tiny plane floats over parchment hills that unravel to our left. We briefly land in the tiny community of Tulita and most of the passengers leave. As we take off again, climb and angle away from the Mackenzie, the shadow of the plane follows as we track the shoreline of Great Bear River heading east.

Peter bends over the tiny fogged-up window and watches the glittering river curve through landscapes he's memorized from archival accounts. He turns and points out the approaching rapids. Between his knees is the bucket of Kentucky Fried Chicken the band representative asked us to pick up in Yellowknife.

SIX

Déline Airport is one small room, bustling with greeting. A tiny blonde in a bulky parka waves as we pick up our bags. Deborah Simmons works with the Déline Uranium Team, a group that monitors both the history and the current impact of the uranium mine. She hustles us to a shiny truck and drives us down a bumpy snow-packed road into town. We check into Grey Goose Lodge, the town's only hotel: a dozen rooms, a restaurant, a gift shop and a wraparound porch. Large vehicles idle outside with engines running, exhaust clouding the brittle air. If you turn the motors off they'll freeze and you won't get them going again.

The lodge is the hub for interactions between the community and visitors, the architecture of the North and those invested in it. In February, light is returning, albeit barely. With so much darkness time is organized differently here. There is unrelenting activity; self-government is being negotiated. In addition to the Uranium Team, Déline is home to a Great Bear Management Project, an education committee developing a learning centre, an environmental assessment currently underway, Slavey language classes and a strategic planning session that's about to start.

My room at the Grey Goose is cosy and inviting, with a cheerful rug, a bright bathroom and soft towels. I drop my bags and check my email. My boyfriend is complaining about snow. I type back that it is minus thirty-eight here. Then I join Peter in the dining room. He has already opened his laptop and looks completely at home in this sea of strangeness. It is nice to be travelling with a male friend I don't have to look after.

The room bustles with activity, small groups at each table busy with meetings, making notes and talking on cell phones. I want to ask a completely naive question: What are all the white people doing here? Are the lawyers and legal teams, graduate students and researchers, civil servants and engineers, are all of us reconfigured missionaries of the modern age – the victim industry, disguised as the empowerment industry, outsiders making our livings from the sufferings of others? Or is this a good example of an indigenous community getting what it can from what's available; people from many walks of life bringing the resources we can offer? Why are Peter and I (who are, after all, both white and up here) increasingly irritated and disturbed?

A lanky fellow with wire-rimmed glasses carrying a plate of fries sits down and introduces himself. Kevin has come from Toronto to lead this week's capacity-building workshop. "It promotes empowerment through development," he explains. "I'm here to skill these people up." Peter later takes a photo of Kevin wheeling his smart black suitcase through the twilight, wide streets deep in snow, the open expanse of Great Bear on one side and scattered frame houses on the other. Man against nature, he strides determinedly forward.

Back in my room, the phone on the small bedside table rings. Deb is at the front desk; she has brought warm clothing for Peter and I to borrow. We pile on thick hoods and too-large boots and head outside to visit the *Radium Gilbert*. I feel a combination of travel fatigue, culture shock and the anticipation of coming face to face with a boat that spent years carrying sacks of uranium ore.

We crunch our way single file along the road to the edge of town, past a small cemetery and a cluster of tiny white crosses. The sky is a brilliant blue, the horizon endless. I can't see anything not directly in front of me since it's far too cold to let more than my mouth and nose protrude beyond my massive beaver hood. I experiment with how much of my face I can cover without fogging up my glasses. Not much. Every few minutes I swing my upper body from side to side, trying to get my bearings, then return to stepping carefully into Deb's footprints. The afternoon sun bounces wildly off the blinding snow.

We reach the shoreline and keep walking, out onto the blanketed ice of the frozen lake. Peter takes great pictures, one of which he later frames and gives me. It's a close-up of the hull, and you can see RADIUM G etched neatly in fresh black paint, in the background chipped flakes of the original battered surface. We are lucky to get this visit. A few months from now the old tug will be chopped into pieces and stored near the airport. In two years she'll be taken south over the winter road.

Peter eagerly approaches the boat. I stamp my feet to keep blood flowing and enjoy his excitement, but I stand back. Behind me, grinning behind dark glasses is a young graduate student from Edmonton. "Don't worry," he says, "there hasn't been a trace of anything dangerous here for years!" His name is Jack and he is researching the health of the caribou in the area. He keeps me company while the others show Peter how to climb up to the narrow deck. They move slowly, reminding me of television footage of the moon landings. Peter disappears inside.

Jack speaks but I can't hear – the warm fur hood blocks my ears. I shake my head. He stands directly in front of me and shouts,

"The old-timers talk about powdered dust from the ore bags spilling into the lake! The ore would leak, like fine sand all over people's bodies. If the bags broke, they'd shovel the ore into the water."

It's a guess, but they say one million tons of radioactive tailings ended up in Great Bear Lake, although some were dredged up when the value of uranium was discovered. A health study currently underway will later reveal no harmful effects to caribou or the water.

We walk back to the edge of town and I linger, trying to take in the horizon, imagining what this place was like during World War II. Jack waits for me, and when I catch up to him, I tell him what I'm thinking. "During the war people were afraid the Germans would bomb them," he says. "Germany was close to winning and Déline was so near the mine." I have another photo from that afternoon – Peter, Deb and Jack, bundled head to foot and grinning in front of the *Radium Gilbert*. The old boat's side is scrawled with graffiti.

Before we speak with any of the elders, we have to meet the chief. Deb picks us up after breakfast and we drive by snowmobile down the broad white road, past small houses, stray dogs and a few service buildings that remind me of Florida motorhomes. We park, enter the community centre and remove our outdoor gear. The toasty building is also a hub, but for communications, and is filled with computers and project groups. One of them is the Déline Uranium Team, which is documenting the long-term effects of mining on health in the area; families, land, water, wildlife.

We are introduced as researchers interested in the history surrounding Eldorado. A woman in a yellow blouse looks up from her papers. "Can you find out what happened to my aunt?" she asks. "My mother's sister. She was a teenager when she got sick. They sent her to a hospital in Edmonton." Peter asks if she remembers when this was. "Around 1950. The family never found out what happened. She just disappeared. It wasn't at all unusual."

Peter says he wishes that he could help, but this isn't what he's researching. The woman nods and goes back to her photocopying. Peter heads down the hall toward the chief's office, but I hesitate. Peter is right, we have no idea what happened to individuals and we have never looked at those kinds of records. My impulse is to ask for more information, to drop everything and see what can be done for this woman. I don't know if my confusion is a genuine wish to help or embarrassment that we didn't include tracking down lost relatives in our research goals.

A smiling young woman in a red blazer is talking with Peter. I join them. She ushers us down the hall into a small, sunny office.

Chief Raymond Tutcho appears to be in his fifties, has silky black hair and is not wearing shoes. Neither are we. He asks why we have come. Peter tells him that we see a "kind of southern deficit or debt in relation to the uranium history" that we want to address with our work. He describes the volume of archives in Ottawa, most of which has not been looked at by independent researchers. "The histories written to date are not interested, not even slightly, in the Dene's connection to any of it, and don't mention them as historical actors. Even though much of this is the very documentation the Dene can draw on to support their grievances."

I say I am a storyteller, here to listen. I would like to pass on what I learn here to people in the south, through a play or an opera. We then raise, carefully, the question of speaking with elders. We know that since Peter Blow's documentary there have been journalists and many others arriving in Déline looking for interviews. "We are not ethnographers or anthropologists and we have no formal interview scheme," we say. "We only would like to tell them what we have learned from the historical record, and speak informally with anyone interested and able. That's all."

The three of us sit quietly for a minute. I hear snowmobiles outside. The chief looks pointedly at Peter. "You must be careful with the stories the elders tell you. They do not want to repeat themselves." With that we are neatly and politely ushered out.

"Why would a story only want to be told once? This makes no sense."

It's ten p.m. and Peter and I are in the Grey Goose Lodge, still vibrating from the day's events. There is no alcohol here, officially, and not much nightlife that we can see – everyone staying at the inn has disappeared. Peter offers the Jack Daniels he's brought from his room. I accept. When I drink I ask more questions.

"Is it the stories that don't want to repeat themselves ... or the elders?" He shakes his head. "Or both?" I continue. I open a package of cheese and cut us some slices.

The enigma of the chief's remark and our interest in the Dene's stories about the mine has led us to the circles and layers of things we want to explore. None of this falls under academic disciplinary frameworks. What Peter ends up writing will not be traditional scholarship. What I write will not be "the story of the Dene." Neither history nor journalism, we follow what Peter calls "leakage": the tributaries – material, narrative and memorial – in and around the highway of the atom.

"The chief is giving us a gentle warning," says Peter. "There is a lot to know before we can even approach what we're interested in."

I nod. "So ... what we *think* we're interested in can't be approached directly?"

"Yup. And this is only limiting *if* we cling to the idea that questions are what determine answers. Whereas it might be, a question always gets the answer it deserves." Peter is paraphrasing Deleuze, the Parisian philosopher.

I am wondering if I want to buy moccasins. There are some beautiful ones in the gift shop. Peter leans back in his chair and shuts his eyes. "The 1943 Lord Haw-Haw radio broadcast, do you know what it said? The announcer promised the 'Japs would blast Port Radium and Norman Wells off the map.'"

"Peter, how do you know who Lord Haw-Haw even is? Where do you find these details?"

His eyes remain closed. "Your parents were in radio. You mean you don't know *Germany Calling*, the famous broadcasts from England. What kind of a daughter are you?"

I laugh. "I learned other things from my parents."

He opens his eyes. "What?"

"'The road through this life is like a razor's edge: hell on one side, hell on the other.' George Salverson. He forgot the rest of it."

"Which is?"

"'Between these two runs the road through life.' Rabbi Moshe Loeb, misquoted by George Salverson."

Peter pours me another glass. "The witness always comes too late."

The Band Council started asking to meet with government officials in Ottawa in the late '70s. That was when the men started to die. I have been loaned a few documents, including a Déline Uranium Team (DUT) Mental Health Assessment from July 2002. I'm too restless to sleep, so I read about healing historical trauma, sacred myths and health reports. "Many bereaved attempt to master their losses by seeking out action and activity. However, in order to master successfully a disastrous situation, there needs to be a sense of hope that circumstances will improve." A woman being interviewed asks if she can say a few words at the end about her husband, because she misses him. The perception that restitution will never fully occur, most of all the interminable process of not being listened to, has had a devastating impact in Déline. Chronic distress and dysfunction is the second disaster for the community; unresolved grieving. A missionary interested in Dene surgery wrote in 1901 that people in this community "could tolerate pain extremely calmly and remarkably, provided it was accompanied by the hope of fast relief and recovery."

I once heard an interview with German medical historian Barbara Duden about the knowledge we hold under our skin. She described the changing ways medicine has understood the body. I think what caught my attention, so many years ago, was the thought that my body could speak but I didn't know how to listen. Graduate school later gave me a vocabulary that helped me understand interactions with the world not captured in words. French sociologist Pierre Bourdieu used the term *embodied history* to describe how all of the past is active in the present, not only what we remember or what has been written down. Passions, deep feelings and imaginative guesses are part of creative acts and discoveries. "We can know more than we can tell."[23] This is not the language the Dene are using, but the health report I'm reading suggests that there is much between the lines of what they have to tell us.

"The body can hold what has passed out of mind," writes Canadian geographer Joy Parr.[24] In a study of Canadian communities affected by environmental disaster, she says that we make sense of the world directly through our sensing bodies. This means it isn't enough to ask people what they think about something; it's important to try and find language for what they wouldn't think to tell us, and to pay attention to what doesn't qualify as important. If we want to know a fuller story – be better witnesses – we have to listen to the invisible. Parr realized that most historical studies ask questions about property lost, or physical health. "The grief for which they could not find words is often dismissed as nostalgia,"[25] she writes.

In the DUT report the woman asks to speak about her husband. Because she misses him. I think about the woman at the photocopy machine earlier today who asked Peter if he could find out about her aunt. "She just disappeared," the woman told him. "It wasn't at all unusual."

I switch off the light and wonder what my friend Rosemary Jolly would make of the situation in Déline. She says that back home in South Africa it is not a tragedy to die; rather, it is a tragedy to sever the connections between the living and the dead. It is the disruption of a cosmos that is the loss. A different cosmology than in the west, where there is the binary of living/dead, here/gone.

I'm exhausted from all the interaction and fall into a heavy sleep. It lasts an hour, and then I'm wide awake. The clock says midnight. Curious about the cable television I have heard is so extensive in the north, I check to see what's on. The Déline community station features a series of rotating announcements. I blink, look again, see my name flash by.

Peter van Wyck and Julie Salverson will speak tomorrow night at the community hall. They are experts on Eldorado and uranium mining.

I stare in dismay at the screen. This is a surprise. Nobody told us anything about giving a talk, and certainly not as experts! So much for sleep.

SEVEN

I call Peter's room first thing the next morning. No answer. I switch on the television; the announcement is still there. I notice something else at the bottom of the screen: *the elders will be present*. Great. In twelve hours I am going to speak publicly to the elders of Déline.

The Grey Goose parking lot is full of trucks and the dining room is busy with clusters of people huddled over coffee and eggs. Peter has seen the announcement and has the same reaction as I did. It's fine to speak, but to be called experts? Oh dear. I feel, not for the first time, the sweet relief of being in this together.

We quickly come up with a plan. Peter will tell them that he is interested in nuclear waste, this difficult problem that the US government has attempted to solve by putting most everything on Aboriginal land. He will say that he saw the film *Village of Widows* and thought to himself, this is the beginning of the history of nuclear waste. Port Radium; Déline is really the beginning.

I will tell them about my plays with survivors of violence and my research into how to be a witness. Fortified by having a plan, I polish off a bowl of cereal, grab an apple juice and pull on my coat. I hurry to the elementary school where I have arranged to lead a drama workshop with grade five students, a task that will nicely distract me from the evening ahead.

A month before the trip, I visited a grade five/six class in Toronto and talked about Canada's uranium and its connection to World War II. The kids were fascinated and together we mapped out the route from downtown Toronto to Déline. The class wrote letters to the northern students, which I've brought with me, stuffed into a thick brown envelope. We hope the Déline class will reciprocate.

The wall outside the entrance to the Déline elementary school is painted with a colourful mural of northern lights, caribou and fish. Inside, artwork hangs on bulletin boards and curious children peer at me as they change classrooms. The fifth graders are hard at work at their desks when I arrive, and are full of energy and eager to sit in a circle with a newcomer. For the next few hours, fifteen students create dramatic tableaus and draw pictures about the bush, fishing, skidoos, picking berries, playing with friends and bumper cars in Edmonton. They tell me that they are born here, are Aboriginal and would like to take me camping. I thank their teacher, a competent young woman from Ontario who has been in Déline for one year and will likely only stay one more. She promises to have letters and drawings mailed out and she is true to her word. A month after this, the Toronto students will proudly post letters from their Dene pen pals around their classroom.

As I walk back to the Grey Goose in the gathering dusk, it occurs to me that none of the children have asked me to explain who I am or why I'm here. They simply welcomed me and we played.

I join Peter for supper and we walk to the event. A deep chill has moved in, dropping the temperature to minus forty-two. The sun has set. There is a vague hint of cherry red to the sky and a greenish-blue that someone tells us could turn into northern lights. At the hall, my nerves blow up. I hide in the washroom until there is no reason to keep washing my hands. People arrive, everyone bundled in thick, worn coats with beaver gloves and hats. Women arrange snacks on a long metal table. It is mercifully toasty in this large window-lined room. A film is advertised, but Peter and I are first on the bill. I wonder if it's a courtesy for the out-of-towners, in case everyone leaves after the movie.

The old people settle themselves into black plastic chairs. I notice Jack from the walk to the *Radium Gilbert* waving at me and I'm grateful. A couple of kids play Hacky Sack at the front while the schoolteacher from Ontario sets up the film projector. I eat cookies from a paper plate by the coffee urn and feel my nerves fold up and smooth away. People here are far too concerned with what's happening to their land and their families to bother about me. This evening is no kind of inquisition.

I speak first. I am about to say that I won't write about things I don't know, make an awkward apology for being introduced as "experts," but I stop. I think of Maria Campbell telling Linda Griffiths, "Know your own history!" I remember Lily Watson asking, "Why are you here?" In front of me are the parents and grandparents of the children I've spent the day with. I tell them who I am; I don't use notes. I say I am a storyteller. Often I work with communities that want to use theatre to share who they are. "I am here in Déline to listen and take what I learn back to people in the south. And perhaps make a theatrical performance that tells about this place and what happened here because of the mine." I say that I want to bring information about Port Hope, New Mexico and Japan back to Déline. I go on to tell them my own connection to the story – how I grew up near Lake Ontario not far from Port Hope, where the uranium from the Port Radium mine was processed. People nod.

Then it is Peter's turn. He opens his computer and reads some text he prepared earlier in his room. First, he thanks them for how welcoming and generous they have been, and tells them how beautiful their home is. Then he tells them a story:

I was reading in some old copies of the *Mackenzie Valley Viewer*, where there was a series of pieces called Sahtú Godé Dáhk'é (the Place of Stories). And one that I read that really made me think, recounted by Alfred Masuzumi, was about [a nosebleed and] how the orphan boy outwitted the mean medicine man. The medicine man, in this story, couldn't believe that, with all his power, all his life could drain out of him, one drop at a time. As though something small like blood dripping could kill him.

So I thought about this story for the last couple of days, and it has made me think. . . . It has made me realize that in the south, this story is not understood at all.

It is hard for governments (and some people) in the south to imagine that we are injured *one drop at a time*. But we are. Isn't this how cancer kills? One cell at a time? And isn't this just like how we lose a generation of our young people? One dropout at a time? Isn't this how governments make people poor, by cutting one service at a time?

But fortunately this works in reverse. This is exactly how things get built, one thing, one brick, one idea, one story, one person at a time. Just like your knowledge centre will do . . . one thing at a time.[26]

He tells them about the archive in Ottawa full of photographs and stories about Port Radium, still classified as "secret." Then he talks about the highway of the atom and how huge it is, how it tells the story of the twentieth century. "A century filled with colonial occupation, incredible intolerance, racism and hatred and a staggering amount of killing. And it has left a toxic heritage that we are only now beginning to understand. So, we're all highway workers in a way. But we're at work on different points of the highway of the atom. Your knowledge centre covers this area, the Sahtú. We will need many more. It's an ambitious project, but we must start somewhere. One thing at a time."[27]

Peter takes from his satchel a small bag – a gift.

"I brought you something. It's just a small thing…a portion of the highway of the atom. It's a piece of salt taken from the burial site in New Mexico, where some of your land has been put. You can do with it what you like, but I thought you might put it in your knowledge centre."[28]

When we are finished speaking, the woman moderating asks, "What do you think?" There is quiet for a moment. What I notice most are the faces of the elders: tough, resilient skin, wrinkled like paper folded hundreds of times and then smoothed out. A wiry woman in the front row stands up, leans for a moment on her husband's shoulder, straightens and says, "Let's get on, it's about the future, enough with the past."

The heavy-set man on the other side of her, maybe her father, seems angry, but I can't tell. He gets up, turns away from us to speak to the group. "If you've got something to say, pull it out of your pocket. Otherwise it will rot."

I can't stop glancing at a very old man in a red-checkered hunting jacket leaning against the wall. He stared at me, expressionless, throughout my presentation. Afterwards he walks quickly toward me and I prepare myself for what's coming. He stops abruptly, a huge grin spreads over his face and he grabs and pumps my hand. "Yes, we came tonight to see a film but a presentation is good. We learn. Thank you. We need the information." I am embarrassed to be so relieved. And then, it is as if I see this man clearly for the first time, not clouded by my own projections and fears but as a true stranger who, in his separateness from me, I might now possibly meet.

There are productive tensions at the heart of witnessing. The witness listens for and confirms the familiar, the predictable. I come to Déline knowing there has been illness and loss. But the witness must also be available to surprise – there are some people here who would like to reopen the uranium mine, and some (most of them? All?) do not consider themselves victims. If I don't recognize the assumptions I bring with me as a visitor, I can't change them. I need to be self-aware.

Until now I have assumed that listening is about how I hear the stories of others. I have forgotten that putting myself into the equation is not indulgent; it is necessary to the hope for an exchange with any degree of mutuality. As this Dene elder smiles and shakes my hand, I recognize that I must also witness my own stories. This is something I previously understood only in theory. Now it feels alive in me – an experience, not just an idea. To be available to another person I must first be available to myself.

Witnessing trauma is structured by the terms by which survivors testify. If the victim always speaks through the hierarchy of helper and helped, and the witness listens through this same dynamic, then a patronizing search-and-rescue mission is reproduced. The listener always has more power, and the petitioner seeks the recognition the listener is empowered to grant. Most attempts to seek redress are staged and reported in this way – the helpers grant time, acknowledgement or resources to the helped. The optics of this dynamic maintains the hierarchy and makes communication on equal footing mere window dressing. The victim–helper polarity is entrenched in the exchange itself, whether it takes place in a national courtroom or a private conversation. The roles are assigned culturally and the conversation unfolds accordingly.

How can this hierarchy be undone? Psychoanalyst Dori Laub, one of the founders of the Fortunoff Video Archive for Holocaust Testimonies at Yale University, says that psychic survival depends on our own internal witness – a kind of self-respect. This inner witness is produced by relationships, through interactions with other people. "That is to say, we learn to talk to ourselves – to think – by talking to others. Our experience is meaningful for us only if we can imagine that it is meaningful to others."[29] This happens when we speak and are heard as full subjects. The Dene elder, whose name I never learned, had given me a gift. Like what the women in Soweto offered to Rosemary Jolly, this elder has granted me the status of subject. "To conceive of oneself as a subject is to have the ability to address oneself to another."[30]

After our presentations, Peter and I are invited to have tea. For the next two days, we visit people in their homes. We stop worrying that we don't know enough about the community's history. We bring our willingness to know, our desire to learn how to know, our willingness to have tea.

We are told that the problem with Canadian history is that it has left the Dene out of the story. I need to hear this; my fear of saying the wrong thing might make me do the same. A man who piloted the pitchblende along the river says he got bored more than anything else. "No time to sleep. Current is so fast." Stories are passed down in Déline, what it was like to work at the mine. One of the men's arms always got red and he'd be so exhausted he'd lie down to sleep on the bags. "They used to throw rocks into the lake and if they knew some of the rocks had ore, they would try to take them out again. It was a game."

We are not learning what we expect to learn. We are not hearing information that clarifies the historical record. Why not? It has something to do with the retroactivity of this entire story. Peter later writes, "Things were not remembered clearly because they were not experienced as significant in the first place. Things gained their significance after the fact."[31] Once it became clear that the Dene's land, the mine, uranium, cancer and Hiroshima were connected, a simple job done all those years ago, like loading a boat or packing ore into a sack, became something else entirely.

In these informal conversations, we hear about experiential knowledge contained in stories that make them meaningful. "This is not traditional ecological knowledge . . . concealing perhaps just another discovery narrative, another gesture of cultural conde-scension . . . but listening and thinking and knowing that there is something to be learned that requires effort and willingness."[32]

Peter and I try to be available to what the Dene do not tell us. Stories are power, and the choice of what is or is not shared is deliberate. We read accounts of medicine stories, like the or-phan boy tale that Peter mentioned in his talk. But most of these are not for us to hear. George Blondin writes that "most medicine people don't talk about . . . sacred and secret."[33] This power can be used or abused and was hardly mentioned by early explorers, who couldn't seem to understand why the Dene lived so richly in this frozen place. The first white men to visit Canada's North would never have survived without help from the Inuit and the Dene. "It is perfectly obvious from the record," writes Rudy Wiebe, "that on first encounter with the land of the Dene, the English, despite their extraordinary resolution and courage (or perhaps because of it), were as helpless as infants in arms."[34]

There is a power in medicine stories that speaks not only to how the Dene lived a century ago but to how they live now. The changes the Dene have made in Déline are as invisible to outsiders, and perhaps as private, as the places this community fiercely protects from change. The clues to pay attention to, the way of "sensing changes," as Joy Parr puts it, are found in embodied knowledge.

Each day we are in Déline the temperature drops further. We are invited to go camping overnight, and I'm both relieved and sorry that we are leaving the next day. Perhaps another time. The cold makes walking difficult, so on our last morning, Deb Simmons drives us and interpreter Mark Modeste to a small one-storey home. She drops the three of us off and we are greeted warmly by elders Theresa and Peter Baton, who offer us a seat in their cozy, smoke-filled living room. They each light another cigarette and ask why we have come.

Theresa is an elegant woman, poised and muscular with long, silky grey hair. It is said that women were the strong ones in the bush. She is respected in the community as an intellectual, able to navigate without bitterness between two cultures and two languages. Theresa smooths her floral skirt over her slender knees and offers us molasses cookies. Her husband, Peter, a squarely built Dene man in his eighties, is a former chief who is still consulted about hunting or trapping expeditions. He asks if I have children. I say no and he shrugs and smiles. "Kids are like sled dogs," he confides. "Good ones and bad ones." He laughs like a series of hiccups, lights up another smoke and points a bony finger toward his wife. "Women too! This one, she's very good!"

Peter and Theresa moved to Déline when it was still called Fort Franklin. The uranium mine closed in the early 1960s. Theresa says that when they lived at Port Radium, the women would make tents for their families to sleep in from the sacks that carried the uranium. There has been much illness since then, and many deaths from cancer. The town's surviving elders say the prophet Ayah warned them. These are the same people who still have no word in their language for radiation.

There is a framed photograph of the prophet Ayah on their sideboard. Peter reaches to a small table and picks up the book where elder George Blondin wrote down the story of the famous prophecy. Long ago there was a famous rock called Somba Ké, on the eastern shore of Great Bear Lake, near the Arctic Circle. "Loud noises came from this place," says Theresa. "People were warned to stay away."

As we prepare to leave, Baton insists on lending me his beaver mitts. "These are the best in Déline," he says proudly. It is forty-eight below zero outside. "If you pay attention, you can hear ice crack!" I wave goodbye and we step into the frigid air. The noon sun is bright but gives off no heat. I thank Mark for all his work translating and tell Peter I'll meet him for lunch at the hotel. I head to the cemetery with its tiny white crosses. Sitting offshore in a snowy blanket of brilliance is the *Radium Gilbert*. I pull the warm mitts high up my arms and walk onto the ice of the frozen lake, toward the old boat. Her graffiti-scratched hulk tilts drunkenly in the snow.

That night there is a feast. We sit beside long sheets of brown paper rolled out on the floor of the community hall and eat caribou and potatoes. The meat is too gamey for me; it makes me gag and I'm ashamed. I think about the refined and packaged steaks we barbeque in the city, with no idea where they've come from or how the animal was killed.

After dinner, an old woman named Alice agrees to make me a pair of moccasins. She traces an outline of my foot on brown paper and asks what are my favourite colours.

"Blue and red."

She jots this down, her thin brown fingers not much bigger than the pencil. I write down my address and pay for the paper package that will arrive at my apartment in a few weeks. Alice pushes me outside to join Peter, Deb and some of the others for a walk.

"Look!" Deb shouts as we come to the little wooden fence beside the cemetery.

I zip up my hood and crane my head to see where she is pointing. Streaks of phosphorescent green and yellow zigzag across the sky like tracks of some prehistoric bird. Without warning they dive into blossoms of ultramarine, perfect explosions above our heads. When I return to Déline nine years later, I think that the northern lights were the only thing I understood on my first trip. Peter and I stay as long as we can behind the lodge, staring up like people have done for thousands of years. It's no wonder so many got down on their knees.

Peter and I are up before breakfast is served. After thin coffee and a boisterous farewell in the little airport, we fly west along Great Bear River, tumble through Norman Wells and drop into the lobby of an empty Edmonton Holiday Inn. It's only nine at night, but the restaurant is about to close. The teenage waitress yawns, and I obligingly request a salad. Peter, oblivious to the girl's irritation, orders the largest steak on the menu. The feast arrives and he dives in while I sit miserably picking at bits of dry lettuce. I've missed my last opportunity to dine on prime Alberta beef; I'm starving and the delicious bite Peter offers only makes things worse.

I'm teary, disoriented and depressed. Neither of us feels like talking so we head to our rooms, hoping sleep will fix what is suspiciously beginning to feel like culture shock. Seven hours later, we sit, dejected, waiting for the airport coffee shop to open. It doesn't. We mumble about the tasks ahead of us. I will visit Port Hope while Peter returns to the Yellowknife archives. We catch flights home – Peter to Montreal, me to Toronto. Arriving at my boyfriend's apartment, I find he has forgotten to clean or shop – there is only beer in the fridge. He apologizes and rushes out for groceries while I collapse on the couch. For the rest of the unseasonably cold Ontario winter everything feels overheated, crowded and grey.

Port Radium was reopened as a silver mine in 1963, then closed again in 1982. Today, thirteen years after my first visit to Déline, Alberta Star Development Corporation has extensively staked and test-drilled the area. The company's website describes large uranium anomalies that have never been explored and Alberta Star wants to determine "if there is a potential resource to support the recommencement of commercial production at the mine sites."

Alberta Star's permit was granted with permission from the Déline Land Corporation. It officially expired in 2013, but if the company continues to meet regulatory requirements, its mineral claim will remain in effect indefinitely. Uranium mining doesn't just provoke controversy; it provides jobs.

The Sahtúgot'ine, known for their pioneering self-governance, have undertaken a series of initiatives in land stewardship. This includes clean-up work at the various abandoned mine sites on the lake, as recommended by the DUT report. Still, many questions remain. *They Never Told Us These Things* asks how Ottawa could have knowingly let the Bear Lake people select contaminated areas for settlement during their land claims process in the early '90s. Some Sahtúgot'ine say their families have lost faith in governments and their young people see no future; they believe that their place in the world is poisoned and their children will die. But in 2016, the United Nations Educational, Scientific and Cultural Organization (UNESCO) recognizes Great Bear Lake as a world heritage site and commends Déline for its unique land management. In August 2016 environmental group leaders, politicians and representatives of UNESCO arrived in Déline to celebrate the Tsá Tué International Biosphere Reserve, a place "that is now recognized as an international model of how humans should live with nature."[35] This community has a resilience I wasn't looking for in 2002, or even able to recognize.

EIGHT

The first time I visited Déline there was a numbness about me. I had no conscious idea how potent the storms of my childhood were; instead of addressing them, I transferred my hurt to the injustices around me. I had tried once to write about my own life. In my early twenties, the Globe Theatre in Saskatchewan hired me to help create a show about alcoholism and adolescence. Every day we drove our white van across the open prairie to a minimum-security youth facility – a prison, really – where five or six resentful girls would shuffle into a dark gymnasium. A few hours later, they would be laughing, drawing images and making skits about what they called "our fucked up lives." Day after day, group after group, the pattern repeated. Later, alone in our motel rooms, each of us in the company would write bits of material from what we'd heard that day.

Many of the girls were young, Aboriginal, poor and addicted to alcohol or anger. One night I decided that I couldn't very well ask them about personal experiences with drinking if I wasn't prepared to face my own, so I started to write about my own "fucked up" family. I set my scene at our dinner table, always a tricky and unpredictable place. If the day had gone well my mother would entertain us with fabulous stories, like the time she acted in a steak sauce commercial. The company that made the sauce smothered the meat with motor oil to make it glisten under the cameras, and my mother had to lift a fork full of the stuff to her mouth, oohing and ahhing until the director yelled "Cut!" Mum was the life of the party on those days and I would laugh until my stomach hurt. Nobody had a mother as charming, as much fun to listen to. But when her day had gone badly, if she remembered to cook at all, we sat with her helpless fury, my dad's silence and my brother's stiff acceptance.

I don't remember what I wrote in that prairie motel, but about two pages in I went into the bathroom and threw up. That was the end of that. I didn't try to write anything that personal again until a few years after my first trip to Déline. I had been trying to put words to my experience there but I was stuck. Nothing was coming out. One day I started a story about an adolescent obsessed with nuclear war. Then I couldn't stop.

I have few conscious memories of my early years. I was nervous whenever my father's parents came to visit. Everyone would become tense and I didn't know why. Usually I escaped to a book. Once my grandmother stayed for one of her rare overnight visits. I came home early from a high school party to find her reading at our kitchen table. She must have sensed my unhappiness with my evening because she put her book down, poured us both ginger ales and asked where I'd been. I think she noticed that it was Saturday night, and thought maybe her granddaughter should be off having a good time.

"I hate parties!" I blurted. "I never know what to say." She frowned over her clear glasses and sat quietly. Then she confided, "I never liked parties. I can't do small talk either." She kept her eyes on me and I tried desperately to think of something non-small-talky to say. I couldn't, and she went back to her book. I worried for a moment that I had disappointed her, but then was relieved. To say nothing was better than to say something small. I flushed with this new knowledge that I was a serious person, just like my famous grandmother. She was the first woman to win the Governor General's Literary Award, and she won it twice, for both fiction and nonfiction. She had written all kinds of books. I hadn't read them yet, but at thirteen I was impressed that these books had won prizes. I went to bed thinking that my grandmother could probably write so well because she didn't do small talk.

I decided to embrace my grandmother's love of literature. Stories were an escape to other worlds where I could inhabit glamorous personas. I used reading as an excuse whenever I had to endure something social or uncomfortable or scary. This included having to spend time with small children – I hated being left alone with other people's toddlers. When visiting parents disappeared for a stroll through my mother's spring garden, I would halfheartedly roll a ball across the floor, or comb a doll's hair, feeling miserable and confused. Something mysterious was expected of me. I didn't know how to play. But the more crippling feeling, I think, was about responsibility. I was already learning the seductive power of being the one to help.

I loved my mother's father, who we called Bampa. When he stayed at our house he provided a kind of shelter from Mum's drinking. I could tell that it hurt this gracious gentleman to see his daughter so out of control, so unhappy. Come to think of it, he was one of the first adults I tried to cheer up, the first of a long line of rescue missions.

In 1985, I flew to Nicaragua. The country had ended a military dictatorship by electing a Sandinista government that declared ordinary people its priority. They proved they were serious when UNESCO gave them a literacy award: a nation of children taught their grandparents to read. Nicaragua was being reinvented by a generation of young people; 75 percent of its population was under twenty-five. I was close to that age myself, and I had found a home in the anti-nuclear and solidarity movement in Toronto and was enthralled by the dream of a country rebuilding itself. It didn't hurt that there was – to my young and too innocent eyes – a clear opponent to these ideals. The US had declared an embargo on Nicaragua and was covertly supporting a military Contra attack on the Sandinistas. Everyone on the Left considered this a real David and Goliath story.

My chance to get involved began at Trinity-St. Paul's United Church in downtown Toronto, where I'd gone for a concert. The oval stained glass windows were beautiful, and the concert was terrific, but what really hooked me about the place were flyers about Latin America, disarmament and apartheid. I became a regular after a few tentative Sunday service visits.

I grew up in an agnostic home; to my untutored eye, Christians were either evangelical or simplistic. This was through no fault of my parents. In his youth, my father was engaged to a Catholic from Quebec. He wanted desperately to understand this girl he loved, so he located an old Jesuit priest and studied privately for two years. Dad had a philosopher's grasp of theology, even if he never trusted in belief.

I attempted to enlist my parents in Christianity at the same time that I had persuaded them Nancy Drew novels were literature. I was seven and we had just moved into a new suburb. Local kid culture was closed off to me, so I was thrilled when a neighbour invited me to a Sunday school picnic. I was determined to do everything required of the occasion: clean white gloves, cupcakes provided by my reluctant mother – from a mix, but I messed up the icing so it looked homemade – and fierce attention to bible stories read to us by a pale minister under a majestic maple tree.

What should have been a mild infatuation with the church became my first obsession. When I fall, I fall hard, and Jesus was
reliable. I would pray each night after my parents and brother had
gone to sleep. No matter the chaos of the day, the fights or my parents' moods, Jesus was there. He had lots for me to do and seemed
delighted when I screwed up. I don't remember when this stopped,
but it eventually wore off. My conversion resurfaced briefly when I
was a teenager and would go rowing around a lake near a friend's
cottage, reading the bible and waiting to be called.

The discovery of an activist church in Toronto introduced me
to my first real community. The congregation and their minister
were committed to working through people's differences. Pulled
by impulse and curiosity, excited by political issues, I had accidentally stumbled upon an anchor. Although I didn't understand
it at the time, I had found elders, teachings and a process through
which a person could hold herself accountable. Years later, when
I encountered the Dene apology to the Japanese, my experience
of negotiating a trip to Nicaragua, in the context of a spiritual
framework, helped me begin to make sense of the Dene's journey.
What processes did that delegation from Déline go through? What
teachings did the Dene debate and measure themselves against?

Confronted by the question of whether I wanted to formally
join this church on Bloor Street, I spent months reading about the
great religions of the world. I decided that choosing one was a bit
like getting married: if you were an adult and not already claimed
by any one faith, you had the right to choose for yourself. When I
left the church a few years later, I suffered only mildly the depth of
anger and loss so many Catholics carry with them. But that was to
come later; now, I was in love.

Nicaragua captured me one evening in 1985. The speaker was
pastor Jim Wallis from Sojourners, a congregation of activists
who live alongside the inner-city poor in Washington, D.C. "I am

addressing ordinary people and everyday things; nothing heroic," his manner declared. Wallis was in his thirties and had been involved in the Civil Rights Movement in America. To my new friends and I, thirsty for real challenge and honest struggle, here was someone who not only knew what could be done, but would provide us the vocabulary and methods with which to do it. Wallis told a packed church that love was as strong as the force released when scientists split the atom: that miniscule, that directed, that powerful.

After his talk, my friends and I joined Wallis for beers and he regaled us with plans that American activists were making to send teams to Nicaragua. They called themselves Witness For Peace and their main purpose was to "put their bodies on the line" as an American presence against their government's intervention. Each team would live on the Nicaraguan border for one month. During the Contra War, this was the area that experienced the heaviest fighting. "If Nicaraguans can get shot, Americans can get shot too, and attract international attention while we are at it." I don't think I saw this as romantic, but I'm probably wrong. It seemed the inevitable and frightening conclusion to what I took the gospel to mean, about standing alongside the poor and oppressed. I had found the beginnings of my own moral compass. But I was new to this; my checks and balances hadn't yet formed. I binged on goodness.

A group of us met every Friday night after that. We tried to discern what God meant for us. We weren't stupid; we did not have what a friend of mine calls a "Twinkie Jesus" faith. We read the liberation theologians Juan Luis Segundo and Gustavo Gutiérrez and talked about the "preferential option for the poor." We read Martin Luther King, Jr. We took it all so seriously. I don't remember doing anything fun or in any way frivolous during those years. It was the older members of the group who laughed a lot, in particular some of the priests and nuns. I was too caught up in the intensity of it all to know how to let go.

It's difficult now to imagine how completely this took over our lives. Where were our families, friends and other interests? I have no idea what my job was or even if I had one. The rest of the world didn't exist, for all that we thought ourselves out to save it. The 1984 Summer Olympics were happening in Los Angeles while we spent each weekend praying in an old library on the University of Toronto campus. I took no notice beyond a smug disdain for the meaningless frivolity that occupied the ignorant public, including my family. How could they play games while people in Nicaragua were fighting for their freedom? We didn't know that Los Angeles was the only bid that year; the other interested city, Tehran, held back due to the huge cost overruns from the Montreal games eight years prior. We didn't notice that fourteen Eastern bloc countries boycotted the Los Angeles Olympics and held their own event that summer called, ironically, The Friendship Games. We certainly didn't notice that fourteen Nicaraguan athletes proudly visited Los Angeles to compete.

Thinking about myself during that time is the closest I come to understanding the mindset of young suicide bombers today. I believed that an act of love had the power of an atomic bomb. We were committed to non-violence, but some of us were prepared to commit violence against ourselves to carry out that act of love. We studied and held intense debates about how far we were prepared to go; according to God, or our consciences; I didn't know how to tell the difference. We met with American activist Philip Berrigan. This ex-priest, his brother Daniel and others had served years in federal penitentiaries and were preparing for another civil disobedience action. In each carefully planned, non-violent event they would break into a US military base and pour their blood onto nuclear weapons systems. We talked about doing an action like this in Canada. Most of us were too scared and conflicted to take things further than talk.

I dated one of the leaders in our group. He and I had conversations late into the night about how much jail time was okay if we were to have children. This really was the kind of thing we talked about. He was upset that, were we to have children, I wanted him home more than six months out of the year. Clearly I lacked commitment. I felt guilty but stood my ground. I remember drawing that line, being surprised to discover a small place inside myself to hold on to no matter what others thought. I was almost thirty years old. Most of me had become completely caught up in belonging, in being part of a larger purpose. But inside my anxious, stormy self something was waking up. It was solid and reassuring, and it was mine.

In January 1985, I found myself in the back of a truck on a dirt road winding up a mountain two hours north of Managua. The pungent smells of the tropics felt wonderful. The driver stopped several times to tie up loose bolts with rope. Friends and family took me to dinner before I left, convinced I would die in a Contra attack, but nobody had thought to warn me about faulty trucks, loose wheels or bad roads. We laughed with our new Nicaraguan friends, enjoyed the comradeship and stunning scenery, having no idea that in three weeks we'd be lying awake as two armies approached the tiny village of San Dionisio, our home for the next month.

The village was a good distance from the border where most of the fighting was taking place. We were housed in a large classroom that made up the entire pockmarked school, empty because this was their summer holidays and also a place, as we later learned, where the Nicaraguans could find us in a hurry. Several days after arriving we were taken to see a spectacular coffee farm, bushes ripe with heavy beans ready for harvest. It dawned on us that this centre of economic activity made our location a prime target. We had heard that the Contras were eager to attack coffee farms at production time. Uneasy, but with no chance of changing things, we set about developing a daily routine.

We helped local farmers lay bricks for new houses, carefully preserving buckets of water that were only available when the taps ran – sometimes – for one hour in the morning and one in late afternoon. We made repairs to a playground that members of our group had built the previous year, see-saws and climbing bars copied inch by inch from Scadding Court Community Centre in Toronto. We replenished the few bent nails available in the village with new ones from Canada and visited people's homes when invited.

Visiting was not straightforward. If we had a meal with someone, our hosts were then seen as favourites of the Canadians. We accepted invitations but had to be careful not to eat anything made from milk products; there were high rates of tuberculosis in the area and milk wasn't safe. I learned the art of pocketing anything suspicious when my host wasn't looking; not eating what was offered was the height of rudeness.

We weren't sure what to do when a few families invited members of our group to sleep in their homes. Would it be okay to bestow our presence on one family and not another? Was it fair if only some of us stayed with families? Would that make the other Canadians look rude? A pleasant young minister from Vancouver was the only fluent Spanish speaker among us and he grew exhausted as we sorted through the layers of what was and wasn't appropriate. This may be what finally drove four of us – including our translator – to move our few belongings into four tiny houses and nervously say goodbye to each other as night fell. As we settled in for our first sleep under the protection of our new family, we accepted an act of hospitality that would prove more generous than we could have imagined.

At my hosts' home, narrow cots were set together on three sides of the room – the only completely bricked-in part of the small structure. I slept on a thin mattress with my feet at the heads of a young couple, Jorge and Valentina, and my head by the bed that held two of their three children. The oldest was a teenage boy who, like all the very young men in the village, was hiding out in case Sandinistas came to enforce the necessary army service. Once or twice, late at night, the winsome lad slipped into the house and I had the chance to chat with him – just a word or two, broad smiles, nothing much said. Officially the village had no boys over the age of twelve.

Jorge told me that before the revolution he lived with his family on a large farm and worked for the landowner. They had food and shelter but no freedom. Now they owned their own land but it was a small dry plot of dirt. Food was hard to come by. Jorge had a job as one of the caretakers for the church. Valentina didn't care for the revolution; she no longer had pretty clothes and she had headaches she couldn't explain. We Canadian women tried to think of remedies for her and wondered what could be causing the problem. She was too young for menopause – perhaps the altitude? We met a vibrant young activist, the only female in the village to wear shorts and call herself a Sandinista. "It's confusing for the young men," she told us. "Sandinistas have old Russian and Cuban weapons that don't work. Americans give the Contras reliable guns. Which would you choose?"

A few days after I moved to Jorge and Valentina's home, the village was summoned to church for a special mass. Darkness falls fast in Central America. There were no streetlights as I walked with my host family, only kerosene lamps inside the homes that lined the road. The feeling of urgency built as we hurried past people huddled in doorways. We stopped for a moment at the house of Jorge's friend Luis and they whispered together. I could only make out a few words: *lucha, combates* and *Rio Blanco*. When I tried to listen, the two men stopped talking and Jorge pulled me along, *rapidamente*.

The small church was full. My Canadian friends Marie, Brett and Dan sat across the aisle, each with their host families, looking worried. Sometime that night we learned that two bands of fighters were approaching the village: one targeting the coffee farm, the other hoping to defend it. It was foolish to come together at the church; any place of congregation was a convenient target. But sharing the mass was a simple act of defiance. Their faith and their community were stronger than their fear.

For three days the Nicaraguans tried to find a way to get the Canadians out of San Dionisio. We were told we needed to return to sleeping together in the school. "It is not convenient for us to have to look for you." When I left Jorge's house, he showed me the machete he kept under his bed. I realized it was not only for cutting grain and was glad that he would not have to use it to defend me.

As we waited, my imagination ran amuck. The wild chatter of chickens and birds as I woke at dawn, so delightful during the first three weeks of our visit, now sounded like gunfire and screaming. One member of our group was Chilean. Marguerita had left her home after the violent overthrow of the Allende government in 1973. She told me stories of torture and kidnappings as we prepared beans and corn for dinner by candlelight. Being in Nicaragua had brought back memories she needed to share. I tried to listen and at night tried not to dream. These were the bare bones of a revolution, but whose?

Children traumatized before they can speak are hypervigilant; they jump at the slightest noise. Neuroscience tells us that trauma causes changes in the brain that hinder emotional control, making the child fearful and easy to confuse. "The child adapts to the view of the world imprinted on his biological memory," writes Boris Cyrulnik.[36] "Posttraumatic psychic life is thus filled with . . . an acquired hypersensitivity to a kind of world that will characterize our life from now on."[37] If I had understood how childhood shapes our responses my experience in Nicaragua might have been different. Perhaps I could have used Cyrulnik's strategies of resilience to discriminate between the present and the past. "When the trauma is flagrant and hyperconscious, we suffer from the blow but are as yet ignorant of the meaning that will be assigned to it in our personal history and in our surroundings."[38] What happened in Nicaragua was terrifying in its own right, but my ability to read it was flooded with mixed messages. This was not the first time I had waited for an attacker.

Early one morning, we were told there was a truck. We huddled together fifteen minutes later as we rode down the mountain. No time for goodbyes. My friend Marie shook and cried. I was silent. Two hours later, we arrived in the city of Matagalpa. We marvelled at running water and a restaurant with flowers on the tables. We sat in a fancy bar with bookshelves and cheerful people acting normal. I thought of the machete under Jorge's bed. I thought of Valentina's headaches. At midnight we walked through a carnival and watched children ride the Ferris wheel. The firecrackers sounded like gunshots.

When I came home from Nicaragua in 1985, I could no longer talk about heroes or villains or politics; I could only say what I had experienced of the struggles and triumphs of ordinary people. But nobody wanted that. I had invitations to speak at political rallies, but when I was unable to provide tales of revolutionary triumph, I was soon replaced with more activist comrades.

When I came home from Déline in 2002 I began noticing something that reminded me of my post-Nicaragua experience. All I had to say was that the Dene had gone to Japan to apologize, and the person I was talking to was stopped short. It wasn't so much the kind of awe this part of the story produced – I had reacted in exactly the same way. But there was a glassy-eyed romanticism about it that made me increasingly uncomfortable. "Woe to those who need heroes, for they are struggling to mend themselves in imagination," writes Cyrulnik.[39] The more I told people what I was writing about, the more it seemed they wanted to see the Dene as either heroes or victims. I needed to be careful I didn't do the same.

It was time to talk to Peter Blow, director of the 1998 documentary *Village of Widows*, the film that launched Peter van Wyck and I on our journey. He had visited Déline and accompanied the delegation to Hiroshima; surely he would fulfill my need for a less starry-eyed perspective on the Dene. Blow, who left the United Kingdom as a young man, was now in his sixties. When I visited his lush and humid garden in Peterborough, Ontario, he made me an iced tea like the Englishman he is. An obvious storyteller, his voice rings with enthusiasm as he describes how he wanted elder George Blondin to talk on camera in Japan about the prophet Ayah.

"Here they are, having a native prophet, having your own guy instead of these bloody missionaries – it was like getting back to things that could really matter. But George went on about Moses in the bulrushes!" Blow laughs and waves his hands in the air. "I'd take him aside and say, 'George, tell them about the Grandfather!' He would nod. And then, next opportunity, the camera would be rolling, someone would ask him a question, and out came the Moses story again!"

Peter Blow is proud of the movie that major broadcasters wouldn't put on the air. Of all the films he has made over the years, *Village of Widows* is the one that people ask about. He has lots of stories, footage he may someday use in a longer documentary. He put some of it on hold when a group of white families from Alberta told him that they were bringing a class action suit against the Eldorado Mine. As far as he knows, nothing has come of it. "There used to be a group of patients who met every Wednesday. If you want to know about the white miners, go to the cancer wards of the Edmonton hospital."

Before I turn off my tape recorder, I ask the question that brought me here. "Why did they go to Hiroshima?" He reaches down to scratch the golden retriever panting under a peony bush. "Going to Japan wasn't for the Japanese. I mean they're not being selfish or anything, but they go for their own healing." He sits back in his lawn chair and thinks for a moment. "You heal yourself when you address something which you feel. That Dene woman said it so well on camera: 'We didn't know what it was, but we're sorry for the people over there and we want them to know.'"

The last time Blow was in Déline, a healing ceremony took place at the house of the prophet Ayah. Two men, one Dene and one Inuit, had known each other for years. Both were connected by lineage to the 1771 massacre at Bloody Falls. I have never heard of this, so when I get home from my visit with Blow I do a little digging.

Samuel Hearne was a British citizen who travelled the Coppermine River to the Arctic Ocean in 1771. The twenty-four-year-old Hudson's Bay Company employee was seeking a legendary "metal river" that might make a place for a settlement and reveal a passage out of Hudson Bay into the Western Ocean. Hearne was the only white man travelling with the guidance of Chipewyan Chief Matonabbee. There is an account in Hearne's diaries of the massacre.

Matonabbee and his men wanted to reach the Coppermine River so they could attack a group of Inuit. When they arrived, the Coppermine Indians surrounded the sleeping Esquimaux. Twenty-odd men, women and children fled their tents, naked and unarmed. According to Hearne, the attackers enjoyed their work and prolonged the suffering of their victims. The young Englishman never forgot the horror of the scene. He was particularly stricken by the agony of a young girl. Pierced by spears, she grabbed Hearne and twisted herself around his legs. He begged the men to kill her. They did.

Bloody Falls was declared an historic site in 1978 and is part of Kugluk Territorial Park in Nunavut. There is controversy about how white scholars tell this story. For my purposes, it is a reminder that all of us are connected to the angels and devils of history. Rudy Wiebe addresses this shared capacity for violence in *Playing Dead: A Contemplation Concerning the Arctic*:

> There is a further matter of history here, of northernness which we need to be clear about. The European entry into the western hemisphere and the Christian encounter with native inhabitants was, generally speaking, violent. At the same time, the Europeans dragged all their national wars and hatreds onto this continent, wars both political and territorial (as between the French and the English) and commercial (as between the Hudson's Bay and the North West trading companies), and religious (Roman Catholic and Protestant). These imported conflicts often become all the more violent for the distance from "home" and "law" and "public opinion" at which they were carried on. But there also was plenty of violence and brutality and hatred native to North America. To speak of Arctic Canada only: no more before than after Europeans arrived was there a great deal of "noble savage" paradise discernible here.[40]

Wiebe goes on to directly address the events at the mouth of the Coppermine: "If we are using history (as we must) to try to understand our present world, then in all honesty we cannot ignore the data which history presents, though it might be suitable to our present purpose to forget them. Racial conflict in Arctic Canada is not now all white versus native, and it never has been."[41]

Peter Blow tells me that the two young men in Déline, descendants of both sides of this conflict, created a ceremony at the house of the prophet Ayah, the Grandfather. "They had been in a rock band or something together, and even as far back as college or university they would josh each other about this. They were buddies and said, 'You know what? We have to make that peace.'" A cynic might say that the apology in Hiroshima was about politics. "That would be fair enough," says Blow. But the ceremony between these two young men was something else altogether. "When you actually see something that has nothing to do with anybody, is just the locals, then you see it as a real cultural template. They really look to make these healing things."

For the sangoma of South Africa, healers and practitioners of *ngoma*, spirits in the body travel different routes and carry a person's history. When that spirit, or history, is blocked – not told – illness occurs. The process of writing this book is becoming my response to the illness that gripped me when I first learned of the Dene apology. As I make sense of my own life, I am better prepared to witness the lives of others. But not everyone agrees that my experience is relevant to the larger story. I have my own anxieties about writing a memoir, and one day they are made explicit. One evening, while working on this book at a renowned writing program, I had dinner with one of the instructors. "You were accepted because your book tells the inspiring story of the Dene apology. Don't bring yourself into it or you will ruin your reputation." I'm stunned, but not completely surprised. I had set out to write a scholarly exploration of the Dene apology. But an author doesn't really control her own book. When I started writing, I could only speak through the lens of my own life. And, as I was told repeatedly in Déline, the prophet Ayah's words of warning aren't just for the Dene. They are for all of us.

NINE

At the National Atomic Museum in Albuquerque (now the National Museum of Nuclear Science & History), sterling silver earrings are for sale in the shapes of Little Boy and Fat Man, the two bombs dropped on Hiroshima and Nagasaki. When they were first sold in the museum's boutique, Japanese tourists complained and the earrings were removed. They're back when Peter and I visit in February 2004, displayed on the shelf with other assorted souvenirs. I buy a pair, thinking nobody will believe me otherwise.

I'm excited to be in New Mexico. The state has a mythic quality. I imagine Georgia O'Keeffe landscapes as we drive out of town in our rented white Pontiac following signs for Highway 20 North. We head for Los Alamos, home of the Manhattan Project and the scientists who worked on the atomic bomb from 1943 until well after the end of the war.

The Manhattan Project was the culmination of decades of work by scientists and the opportunity of a world war. Italian physicist Enrico Fermi was the first to artificially generate radioactivity in

1934. He and his colleagues in Rome discovered that the radioactivity of a metal was one hundred times greater when the neurons bombarding it were slowed down by water or paraffin – an experiment successfully performed in a goldfish pond.

Hitler's increased aggression in Europe brought with it the fear that Germany would succeed in creating the first atomic bomb. In December 1938, Berlin chemists Otto Hahn and Fritz Strassman bombarded uranium with neutrons and identified barium in the residue, "splitting" the atom and creating nuclear fission. Hahn, bewildered by the results and worried about the Nazis, wrote to his colleague Lise Meitner, an Austrian Jew in exile in Sweden. She was able to articulate, in the first theoretical explanation of nuclear fission, what had happened in the lab in Germany.

Hahn was captured and taken to England in 1942 with eleven other German scientists. Cleared of any involvement in developing weapons for the Nazis, Hahn was in custody on a farm near Cambridge when he learned that the atomic bomb had been dropped. The fifty-six-year-old chemist was stricken by the news, convinced that his discovery of fission had contributed to the carnage. Meitner, still in Sweden, was later invited to join the Manhattan Project but refused. During World War I, she had developed X-rays on the front lines and the experience had given her a taste of the horrors of war. She wrote in her journals, "I refuse to answer death with death." When I write the libretto for my atomic opera, Meitner is a central character.

In 1942, control of atomic research in America was transferred from scientists to a Military Policy Committee with the informal code name Manhattan Project. Barely a dozen of the one hundred and thirty thousand people eventually employed understood the scope of the project. Only a few knew that it was about developing an atomic bomb. Many of the scientists and their families lived in the remote mesa town of Los Alamos. The research was carried out in secret on the site of the former Los Alamos Ranch School, whose program had been based on the Boy Scouts of America. Physicist Robert Oppenheimer, who owned a ranch near Santa Fe, spotted the school and proclaimed it the perfect spot. This is where Peter and I are headed.

New Mexico has one of the largest uranium deposits in America. In the Northwest Territories, the Dene story is intimately bound to uranium. In New Mexico, this dubious honour belongs to the Navajo. These indigenous people say that holy wind – *ních'i* – is responsible for the life, motion and speech of all living things. Small ních'i sit at their ears, advising them on what path to follow through life. Those who repeatedly ignore this advice are abandoned by their ních'i.

The Navajo also teach about listening. The spirits swirl around you, urging you to shift direction. Walk this way, one whispers. Another pushes you off track. The ideal is a balanced and appropriate path through life. It is the wind that gives life. When this ceases to blow, we die. In the skin at the tips of our fingers we see the trail that shows us where the wind blew when our ancestors were created.

The sun spreads heat over low hills. I pull out the map. If we turn west on Highway 40, in just over one hundred sixty kilometres we will reach Church Rock. This small community sits on some of America's richest and most extensive uranium deposits, which is why the Navajo and their neighbours have been tangled in a legal battle since 1994. This is when Hydro Resources Inc. first attempted to open three uranium mines on their land.

New Mexico was heavy with uranium mining from the 1950s until the 1980s, but there have been no active mines since the last one closed in 1990. That was the year the US Congress passed the Radiation Exposure Compensation Act, to provide payments to sick underground miners and the families of men who died from lung cancer and other respiratory diseases. In 2000, President Clinton extended compensation to miners above ground – millers and other uranium workers.

Rodeo judge and calf roper Mitchell Capitan lives with his wife, Rita, on the Navajo reservation near Church Rock. The couple thought that uranium mining was a thing of the past until they opened their local newspaper one Sunday morning in 1994. To their astonishment, they read that the Nuclear Regulatory Commission had granted permission, without public hearings, for a Texas company to begin a process called "in-situ leach" mining – not blasting, but pumping uranium out of the ground. The ground in question happened to be a pristine aquifer, the sole provider of drinking water for approximately fifteen thousand people.[42]

I don't know any of this as I contemplate the New Mexico map, enjoying the warm wind through our car's open windows. It is years later, as I search for newspaper reports of the Church Rock confrontation, that I discover how familiar Mitchell Capitan was with the technology of in-situ leach mining. In the 1980s, he was a lab technician on a pilot project for Mobil Oil. "No matter how hard we tried we could never get all the uranium out of the water, so Mobil gave up. We closed the project." I don't know it in 2004, but Rita and Mitchell lead their community through a process that will culminate in a court case at the Supreme Court. And they will lose. The highest judges in the land grant this company the right to begin mining on November 15, 2010.

There is a Japan connection in this story, too. Hydro Resources Inc. is a subsidiary of the publicly traded corporation Uranium Resources, who is in partnership with one of Japan's largest corporations (Itochu) to evaluate and develop the Church Rock site. Within months of the 2010 court decision, the world will be reeling from an earthquake and tsunami that puts Japan and the Fukushima reactor on every Facebook page, screen and newspaper on the planet. But that's a long way from this quiet morning in the New Mexico sunshine.

It is well past lunchtime when Peter and I drive along a high ridge and enter Los Alamos. The town is high in the Jemez Mountains, and I can smell snow and pine trees. The home of the Manhattan Project sits in the remains of a much earlier explosion; nearly one million years ago, a *super volcano* erupted. These impressive mountains were left behind.

Peter parks the car and checks out an information centre while I stretch my legs and photograph the street sign: Oppenheimer Avenue. There are birds everywhere, and I wonder if one is named after this mountain plateau, Pajarito. The Japanese call one kind of origami *pajarita*, or "little bird." Origami are traditional paper figures, like those folded by Sadako, the Hiroshima schoolgirl who died of radiation poisoning. Peter emerges with coffee and directions to our first official destination: the Black Hole of Los Alamos and its larger-than-life director.

Ed Grothus used to work at the Los Alamos National Laboratory (LANL).[43] We meet him in a cavernous warehouse packed with aisles of atomic memorabilia. A solid man of eighty-one with a shock of thick white hair and vivid blue eyes, this custodian of nuclear memory wears camouflage pants, a tie shaped like a nuclear reactor and a large Peace button. He offers us coffee and jokes that the drink is probably radioactive. "I walked in a peace march in the sixties so they fired me," he announces with a loud laugh. Peter and I aren't sure if this is another joke.

Ed continues his autobiography as he pours strong black coffee into big yellow cups. "I came to the lab as a machinist in 1949." He left because he opposed the Vietnam War. It was 1969 and Grothus couldn't stomach spending any more of his precious days "helping build a better bomb." In the early '70s, Ed bought a piece of property that included a supermarket, a parking lot and a Lutheran church. He began to visit the auctions where LANL sold off what they didn't need. Then he started to buy.

For thirty years, Ed has been shelving, packaging and storing everything from missile parts to protective clothing to employee badges (I still keep one of the badges on my dining room bookshelf). Ed's five acres contain millions of salvaged traces from the Los Alamos laboratories, shards and mementos of this country's tortured history. What Ed keeps in his backrooms isn't just scrap. He protests loudly when people call Black Hole a junkyard.

When Yale Professor Shoshanna Felman and Holocaust survivor and psychoanalyst Dori Laub tried to figure out the relationship between trauma and bearing witness, the word they used was *testimony*. Testimony is what Ed Grothus is all about. Felman and Laub wrote the 1992 book *Testimony: Crises of Witnessing in Literature, Psychoanalysis and History*. Their work became an important resource for mental health professionals, scholars and historians confronted with the residual traumas of the twentieth century. In the aftermath of fascism and genocide, what is to be done? What is to be thought?

Felman and Laub say testimony is about an occurrence that is so beyond comprehension it shatters any means we have of making sense of it. It is about an event that blasts into the consciousness of those who witness it. Testimony points not only to evidence, like the kind of testimony that stands up in court, but also "bits and pieces of a memory that has been overwhelmed by occurrences that have not settled into understanding...events in excess of our frame of reference."[44] An acute trauma is a kind of psychic explosion. Ed Grothus, with his boxes of memory, counts as a witness. His twenty years at the LANL anoints him with the sickness of one who knows.

I'm sorry we can't stay until Sunday, when Grothus will dress in scarlet cardinal's robes and perform what he calls a "critical mass" in his reconfigured First Church of High Technology. Grothus has built himself a confessional for the American nuclear conscience. Every day he stages the speech, the anguish and the accusation. He plays Peter and I videos of recent army pep talks. Officers say, "No matter how much damage they do to us, we'll get them," and, "You get people's attention when you threaten the existence of their nation." Grothus tells us to visit the Bradbury Science Museum and see the mock-ups of the bombs dropped on Japan. We do, and it's interesting, but nothing like Ed's mausoleum. When we leave, Ed gives me a gift – two small bits of twisted metal from a box of odds and ends.

That night, I discover in the side pocket of my suitcase a book I forgot I had packed. Debra Rosenthal published *At the Heart of the Bomb: The Dangerous Allure of Weapons Work* in 1990. From what Ed has just told us, the military is still talking the same talk. In Rosenthal's book, a director of civil defense – for a city not far from our motel – speaks at a public forum organized by local citizens. He stands before a huge map of the city and places the tip of his pointer on the intersection of Highways 40 and 25. He tells the crowd that the military believe the Soviets will drop two bombs and points to yellow circles on a map of their town. "Survivors outside would be told to drive north to Santa Fe and take shelter in the basement of the open-air opera house. They would be fed by local restaurants."[45]

Peter and I take the Turquoise Trail south. Peter wants to try out his new camera; I'm glad for a break. Rosenthal's book has depressed me, and I'm afraid that for all Ed Grothus's passion and commitment, his Black Hole is a voice crying out in the wilderness.

Atomic Ed died almost five years to the day from our visit. He was eighty-six and going strong, despite the cancer that killed him. Grothus's comedic irony balanced his prophetic fury. The combination made him a witness who harnessed the ancient power of the fool. In the *Bulletin of the Atomic Scientists*, less than two months before Ed died, Hugh Gusterson compared Grothus to the jester in *King Lear*. "Lear's court jester had a special license to mock because he played the fool. His apparently nonsensical statements often carried the whiff of traitorous frankness. Statements that would have had a courtier sent to the execution block were tolerated from a lowly jester."[46]

Our car winds past family farms that look like they can barely support a few chickens, but many sport a statue of the Virgin Mary. Catholic statues are everywhere here. They seem well tended, if weathered. Most have garlands of flowers thrown over Mary's neck or a bouquet laid at the feet of a chipped wooden Jesus. Like makeshift memorials at traffic accidents, these are glimpses of personal testimonies, awkward attempts to make meaning or fashion someone, or something, that listens.

The weekend before flying to New Mexico I celebrated Valentine's Day with friends in Los Angeles. My boyfriend and I had separated a month before and dinner with similarly single Americans was the perfect antidote for my breakup blues. I told the group that I felt ridiculous, languishing in post-split melancholy while preparing to visit a nuclear storage site and reading about atomic fallout. Who was I to be depressed? "Tell us your battle stories!" they urged. "Trauma only heals when there is a witness. We'll be your witnesses!"

They were joking – they knew about my work in trauma studies and wanted me to lighten up. I laughed and changed the subject. But they were right. The first rule of thumb in the mourning process is the presence of a listener. Someone must be willing to help the survivor create a story that names what has happened – betrayal, grief, loss – but doesn't stay there. Eventually the recycling of pain must shift or the victim stays stuck. To move forward and rejoin the world of the living, to become a survivor, the injured person must take hold of the past and work through it – rework it into an inner self-image distinct from the injury. This is what Freud means by working through loss.

I had spent the last month pondering why I'd fallen in love with another charming alcoholic. After ten days of bruised introspection, I realized I'd been trying to rescue my mother. If I could stop boyfriend A, B or C from drinking, I could keep Mum from ruining all our lives. Then she would stop blowing up and pay attention to me. I was happy to share this discovery with the Los Angeles dinner party, but I couldn't tell them what I really felt about both my breakup and my sad mum. Like many traumatized children, I had a ghost in my closet, a private secret. It had all been my fault.

Family secrets hide inside us, sometimes for generations, like the old stone chambers that used to lie beneath burial grounds. As we drive down an open highway toward the southeast corner of the state, I ask Peter for a good theory about grief. He tells me about a dream described by psychoanalysts, a nightmare common to a person ill with mourning.

"I stand at the edge of a gravesite. I am accused. Here, where I stand, is the site of my terrible crime. Someone stands beside me, someone who is charged with disinterring and examining the remains. This person is accusing me. I don't know who it is. I see a crypt, a tomb. There is an inscription, I bend to read it. The writing is indecipherable. I am accused."[47]

I have always found comfort in making meaning out of anxiety and this brief exchange helps. I fall asleep and don't wake up until the car pulls into a cheap motel near the Carlsbad Caverns, an underground national park. We check into our rooms and soon I'm hearing Glenn Gould playing Chopin through Peter's open door. I lock my room, walk behind the motel into the purple hills and think about the next day, about putting on a miner's cap and taking an elevator a kilometre underground. I think about cancer and gamma rays, and wish I were writing instead about eating and drinking across Italy.

We hit the road as the sun comes up and suddenly, in the middle of scrub desert, there appears the Waste Isolation Pilot Plant (WIPP), advertised as "the world's first underground repository licensed to safely and permanently dispose of transuranic radioactive waste." This includes all kinds of things, like lab coats and instruments that are contaminated by radioactive materials and have a half-life longer than twenty years. The WIPP is surrounded by kilometres of fence and wire. We check in at the gate, park the car and are met by a thin engineer, a public relations guy and a young indigenous man with a briefcase and a crooked smile. They sit us down in a boardroom and give us a two-hour briefing: what to know before going down the elevator shaft.

Radioactive waste comes here by truck from sites across the United States – a huge choreographed dance number. To get a truck into the WIPP, you need to jump through a series of bureaucratic hoops. "We're held hostage by politics," says the public relations guy.

"Things don't go wrong at the WIPP," says the engineer. "If they do, there are controls." When you get "occupational exposure," you'll hear one of three types of alarms ("bell, yelp or gong"), at which point you move to the colour-coded staging area. You have to be over eighteen to visit the WIPP. You sink more than six hundred metres, travelling fast in a tiny elevator, passing through forty-two square kilometres of fossilized coral reef; millions of years ago this area was covered by ocean. Each drum of waste is wrapped in layers of lead and dropped slowly into one hundred million cubic metres of salt, one of nature's most stable compounds.

"Salt," he concludes with a confident nod, "is the most stable compound in the world. Mother Nature keeps it safe."

I used to have a romantic attachment to nature. My family would borrow a friend's cottage in Eastern Ontario and we'd spend evenings on the dock listening to the territorial call of the loons. One summer, I lost my innocence regarding this Canadian icon. I was camping alone on a quiet lake when a mottled brown mallard and her ducklings paddled by single file, a stone's throw from my tent. A moment later, a single white-throated loon floated around the corner of the offshore island, stared unblinking at the intruders, then dove out of sight. For a moment all was calm – a perfect summer vacation postcard. The ducklings paddled behind the mother, their path a thin slice across the water's surface. Suddenly there was a violent splash and the large loon surfaced. She scattered the babies, dove again, then shot into the air beak first, skewering the tiny bird bodies – one, two, three – tiny explosions in the wind. It was over in a second, the loon gone, the mother duck frantic, circling and calling in bewilderment.

The elevator plummets through the earth. We step out into a long tunnel bustling with workers, their hard hats eager spotlights in the dull blackness. I put my hand against cold wet walls of salt. The engineer continues his story with enthusiasm. There are three or four trucks on the American highways at a time, travelling with their precious cargo. Two guys on board and they stop every 250 kilometres for a complete two-hour inspection. The drivers are all in their forties or fifties and can have no violation; they know what they're doing. Any weather event, the trucks are parked.

There have only been two "road events." The one they tell us about involved a nineteen-year-old with a six-pack of Corona. The kid's Toyota hit the back of the truck, flipped it at some rural intersection in a not-to-be-mentioned state. Apparently there was no damage, and, they tell us, the beer was okay.

At the motel, we look through Peter's digital photographs. Most chilling is the black-and-white image of the canisters of waste: six large white garbage cans stuffed with small metal tubes bound together by a shiny plastic-like material. The tubes stick out the top and are capped with oddly shaped tops. The containers are scrawled with numbers and letters –.0.5, SRO, 100, 109 – and rest on a floor of fine salt, buried far below the desert sand.

The first shipment of transuranic waste arrived at the WIPP on March 26, 1999, at 3 a.m. Eighty percent of WIPP employees were there to greet the truck. In nearby Carlsbad people came out on the streets to cheer.

As I write this, high-level waste is back in the news. In 2009, a *Globe and Mail* article said there was approximately forty thousand metric tons of radioactive waste stored at sites across Canada and the "search for a nuclear graveyard" was on.[48] In America, Yucca Mountain in Nevada was meant to be the first repository for spent nuclear fuel rods and solidified high-level radioactive waste, but in 2010, President Obama cancelled the plan because no study found it suitable. On May 16, 2011, two months after the Fukushima nuclear disaster in Japan, a Blue Ribbon Commission of experts appointed by President Obama called for the "expedited" creation of one or more consolidated interim sites for storing the more than seventy thousand tons of spent fuel currently at reactor sites. Most high-level waste in America is stored where it was produced. It's homeless.

TEN

It is a distinct pleasure for me to announce ... that Canadian scientists have played an intimate part, and have been associated in an effective way with this great scientific development.
– C. D. Howe, on the dropping of the first atomic bomb[49]

My father was a writer for radio and television. He couldn't serve in World War II because he was deaf in one ear but he wrote radio scripts full of government-dictated propaganda. My father's briefings were probably supervised if not authored by Ottawa Minister of Munitions and Supply C. D. Howe. One day, Dad showed me a file he'd held onto for over fifty years, containing blue sheets of paper in faded type with official Ottawa letterhead and a list of what must be included in each broadcast. I wish I'd asked him how he felt about this. Was he proud to have done his part for the war effort? Or was he humiliated to have had to follow instructions from an invisible bureaucrat in the nation's capital? He was pleased, I think, that his daughter was asking about his early life.

My father took my brother and I to all the World War II movies. I was six when the Hollywood blockbuster *The Guns of Navarone* was released. I remember holding tight to Dad's big hand as Gregory Peck and Anthony Quinn hauled themselves by rope up a steep cliff in the dark of night, risking certain death from a German gun or the raging ocean below. This was our favourite film. As we watched the dashing American and the exuberant Greek, my imagination was captured. Peck, Quinn and Hollywood itself stood for everything heroic and glorious about the fight for justice.

Alistair MacLean's 1957 novel *The Guns of Navarone* was set on the Greek island of Navarone. The plot was a fiction and Navarone didn't exist, but that hardly mattered. Dad never spoke of his real experience during that war; I doubt it would have occurred to him and I never asked. He was an old-school documentary writer; he believed that his opinion and his story were irrelevant. There were the facts, and then there was Hollywood. Both were necessary and both had their place. There was no reason to mix up good, inspiring fun, which was hard to come by, with truth – impossible to escape.

Canada's entry to World War II was straightforward. By 1939, Prime Minister William Mackenzie King had the dubious distinction of being the only western leader who had met with Adolf Hitler on German soil. Despite Mackenzie King's mystic conviction that the new leader would transcend Nazism and raise his desperate country into spiritual and material enlightenment, Hitler invaded Poland and Mackenzie King was forced to mobilize Canada. In September, Parliament voted to follow Britain. For the second time in two decades, Canada was at war with Germany.

Mackenzie King was re-elected in 1940 with a massive majority that supported his war policies. Not long after that, he signed a tripartite A-Bomb Project agreement with British Prime Minister Winston Churchill and American President Franklin D. Roosevelt. A committee was set up to deal with developing the atomic bomb.

In 1942, Munitions and Supply Minister C. D. Howe secretly nationalized the Eldorado uranium mine on Great Bear Lake. His responsibilities included providing resources, including uranium, to the Allies. Additionally, he offered Alberta as a test site for the atomic bomb. The Americans opted for New Mexico instead. In

October 1945, Mackenzie King wrote in his diary: "How strange that I should find myself at the very centre of the problem, through Canada possessing uranium, having contributed to the production of the bomb, being recognized as one of the three countries to hold most of the secrets."[50]

The Soviets had their own sources of information, one of which was a famous atomic spy with a Canadian connection. Quaker Klaus Fuchs had a Ph.D. from Bristol and was studying in Edinburgh in 1939. When World War II broke out, all German citizens in England were taken to internment camps. Fuchs went by ship to Quebec. He was released eight months later when physicist Max Born wrote a letter on his behalf. In 1943, Fuchs went to Columbia University to work on the Manhattan Project. He arrived in Los Alamos in 1944. In 1945, Fuchs passed on everything he knew about the atomic bomb to a Soviet agent. After Fuchs's arrest in England in 1950, the scientist revealed what he had done and why. He believed that if both major powers had the bomb, then nobody could use it, and that if he didn't act, humanity would always be in danger from nuclear weapons. After a confession and a ninety-minute trial, he served nine years. Fuchs's father said his son had found his own way "out of a situation that seemed hopeless. Neither he nor I have ever blamed the British people for his sentence ... Which of us can be certain how we would have decided in a similar situation?"[51]

In 1948, Hollywood came calling on Eldorado and this Canadian story. A man from Los Angeles was discovered in a newspaper office in Toronto. He was copying the available Eldorado files. The employee who stumbled upon this curious stranger wrote to C. D. Howe in Ottawa:

> I am dropping you this note, as the matter seems urgent. A month ago a man named Aherne, from Hollywood came in

our office in Toronto [*Northern Miner*] and represented as
having your blessing on the writing of a scenario for a movie
on the life of Gilbert LaBine and carrying on the story to the
atom bomb.

Yesterday I ... found Aherne and a young lady had been
copying our complete Eldorado Files. They had been at it
for some days. As they were still far from finished I decided
to leave them alone and see someone in Ottawa about their
bona fides for it seemed to me they were doing a lot of work
to get the background on Eldorado. When uranium became
so important we destroyed a lot of private information on
Eldorado, but there remains a lot of detail about the mine,
the processes there and at Port Hope, much of which has
been forgotten. Whether or not the files would have value to
unfriendly people I am not prepared to say, but I would imagine they are the most complete outside the Company itself. I
will leave it to you as to what if anything should be done.[52]

Peter and I drive northwest through a snowfall and descend
into Alamogordo, a pretty town where the desert butts up against
sloping burnt hills. It is still desert but in the late February afternoon, there are occasional hints of snow. Alamogordo began as a
railway stop on the way to the rich forests of the Sacramento Mountains. Now it is home to several military projects, including the
German Air Force Flying Training Center, established by the German Luftwaffe in 1996. We drive up a hillside along a curving lane
dotted with cactus and potted petunias until we find the home of
our hosts. Nancy is the step-aunt of one of my students. She wrote
to me a month ago to say that she and her husband could put us up.

A golden retriever bounds up to greet us, followed by a woman
in her fifties wearing an emerald sweater, her poise that of a dancer.
A tall, angular man grabs the dog and gives Peter and I a warm

hello. Nancy and Eric have lived in this area for years. Eric flies for a hobby. He says that for him, flying is a place to be alone. This from a man who lives with endless sand on one side and alpine climbs on the other.

Nancy leads us to a back cottage with terracotta tile floors. Sunlight streams though the windows and I feel a release of tension I didn't know I was carrying. Peter disappears into his room to write to his wife. I close my door and collapse with delight on the fabulous mattress. A real home! I can't remember the route we took to drive here, so I open my laptop and look for a map on the New Mexico Tourism site. I scroll down; there is no mention of military test zones amid the videos of stagecoach rides, golfing and Billy the Kid. I look up events for July 16. Civilians are permitted to visit the Trinity test site only once a year, on the anniversary of the first atomic explosion; however, the only thing listed in the events calendar for that date is a flamenco theatre performance in Santa Fe.

Eric rouses us from our computers and takes us to visit his mother, who lives on a steep iron-red cliff. She gives us presents – amber stones, a plate of Serbian cookies and a bag of trinitite she has kept under her bed since her husband died. Eric, my student warned me, voted for George W. Bush and we wonder how dinner will go. It goes splendidly. Nancy and Eric are delightful. They argue constantly about politics, though with good humour. This is a second marriage for each of them and they have built a good life together. Nancy, a New England democrat, tells her husband that this state is living in the past, that things have to change soon in America.

I stay up after everyone goes to bed. The vibrant welcome and disarming American hospitality I received is in sharp contrast to the empty apartment waiting for me in Toronto. I spend time at the end of each day frantically making notes about the trip – anything to not think about my personal life. I have moved many times. I'm in my late forties and still don't know where home is.

Not only that, this subject matter is getting to me. I checked my email and there was a note from the graduate student of a friend asking, "Are you the trauma lady?" I'm not doing a very good job of researching paradise; maybe it's time to schedule another acupuncture appointment. I can't look at the striking country we're driving through without seeing toxic waste and a burning planet. And it isn't just that. When I walk through the underground Carlsbad Caverns or admire the New Mexico landscape, I'm forced to acknowledge something about myself that I don't like: I'm great in a crisis but not so good at relaxing. I'm reminded of something an atomic pilot once said: "I can solve any problem in the air." Me too, I think. But most of life happens on the ground.

I take my glass of wine and sit under the stars with my cacophony of feelings. The dog has followed, but when she realizes we aren't going for a walk, she slumps onto the patio stones and drops her big head onto her paws. She whines anxiously in her sleep. I can't help.

Nancy is up early the next morning. We drink coffee as the sun blazes into a clear sky. She smiles. "When you got out of the car yesterday you were full of sadness. I wondered why." I sputter a few words about the recent breakup, a lover who called me "obsessed," a series of alcoholic boyfriends. She gives me a look and I shut up. "Forty-eight is a great time to go after your own life," she says.

She tells me about her first husband. "The funniest man I ever met." He could hold the attention of the whole bar, with the familiar drinker's swing to depression when the party was over. "I had to leave. Going forward was terribly hard. You don't know where you're going. You have to find out what you want."

I feel a burst of relief that I don't understand. I want to hug this lovely woman but instead I help her wash up. We talk about the peace movement and discover that we were probably in New York at the same time, for a rally in 1982. Thank God women recognize each other, I think, as I drag my bag out to the car. I fight tears as we drive away.

The desert is breathtaking. I wind down the window and let the smell of sage relax me. I start talking to Peter about my breakup. To my surprise, he listens. As I tell him the story, it dawns on me that my boyfriend left because I didn't put up with his drinking. I had stood up for myself! It was *me* he left, not the fake me I always pretended to be. This thought fills me with happiness. I look over at Peter, as if really seeing him for the first time. "I am such a coward. Next love affair, I'd better be more careful." I laugh. "No more drunks!"

He shakes his head. "Being careful is overrated. You're brave. You keep opening your heart." It's a kind thing for him to say. I begin to see that this terrible grief I'm uncovering is not about my boyfriend – it's just easier to cry about him.

It is a beautiful spring-like February day. A sweet breeze becomes a blustering wind that almost knocks me over when I step onto the tarmac of the tiny missile museum. I marvel at Peter, clicking away with his camera. I hold my hair back from my face as the wind slams into me and stare at what must be thirty US military rockets – tall white cones crowded onto an acre of land, a flock of odd birds stranded in this empty way station.

We hurry to the car and head for our appointment at the Trinity Site. I look at the Little Boy and Fat Man earrings sitting on the dashboard beside a postcard of the desert in bloom. I glance at Peter, the intense morning light reflected in his sunglasses. We drive through a startling landscape toward the atomic test site. Everything speaks to me of the living contradiction that is this terribly beautiful world. The willingness to feel deeply comes with a price. Perhaps this is why we resist feeling at all.

"Do the Buddhists have it right, that all we can do is attend and follow a path of least harm?" I ask Peter. He chuckles. "Which path?" I sigh. Poet Tim Lilburn writes that we don't know how to be in this place that is our home: we are "lonely for what we are." In his essay "How To Be Here?" Lilburn "sleeps in the hills under summer stars"[53] and tries to look at a deer. His attempt at contemplation proves impossible. Contemplative knowing is not about feeling peaceful and relaxed. It is not a "reward for the ferocity of one's romantic yearnings."[54] The state he is talking about – about the deer, about the hill, about the journey Peter and I are on – begins with the conviction that knowing is impossible. Only then can another kind of knowing begin.

I turn my thoughts to where we are headed. I have spent my youth trying to escape a nuclear blast and now, voluntarily, I am driving to ground zero. Something is coming full circle in my life, even if I don't know what it is. Being in this haunted place is a kind of homecoming.

> Seen from the air, the crater itself seems like (looks like) a lake of green jade shaped like a splashy star, and set in a sere disc of burnt vegetation half a mile wide. From close up the lake is a glistening encrustation of blue-green glass 2,400 feet in diameter . . . The crater was buried for security reasons not long after the blast.[55]

White Sands Missile Range is an endless expanse of sand and cactus. Most of what goes on here is secret, including research on terrorism. Somewhere out of sight is a scale model of the building from the Oklahoma City bombing. Scott Zeman, an atomic culture and history professor at New Mexico Tech in Socorro, has arranged for Peter and I to visit the spot where the first atomic bomb was exploded. Scott and an official meet us at Stallion Gate at the north end of the Trinity Site. We nod to the guard and climb into a waiting car. We drive south and then east until we reach a small circular area surrounded by a high wire fence. I walk inside.

Everything is remarkably ordinary. I expected a large crater, but there is nothing like that. From a distance, it is possible to make out a slight indentation in the ground, barely noticeable to the naked eye. Otherwise, this is a quiet corner of desert with flat scrub grass and a low mountain range in the distance. Every July 16, the anniversary of the first test, the area is lined with information booths and snack bars. Today, there is nobody.

Many of the atomic bomb scientists were deeply conflicted about their discovery. After a party celebrating the first test, Oppenheimer saw a colleague throwing up and thought, "The reaction has begun."[56] Three months later, the "father of the bomb" retired as director of Los Alamos and each worker was given a silver pin stamped with a large "A" and a small "bomb." American Vice President Henry Wallace wrote in his diary: "I never saw a man in such an extremely nervous state as Oppenheimer. The guilty consciousness of the atomic bomb scientists is one of the most astounding things I have ever seen."[57]

Physicist John Manley suggested the blast of the Trinity atomic bomb – the first ever – looked like a black rose, its petals unfurling as it grew skyward. In October 1945, a crowd gathered in the Los Angeles Memorial Coliseum to witness a recreation of the bombing of Japan. A mushroom cloud burst from the field to the enraptured cheers of the crowd.

Inside the fenced oval is a twelve-foot stone monument marking the spot where the atomic bomb exploded. Every few feet, tied crudely to the wire, are black-and-white photographs: the blast, the farmhouse where the scientists stayed, an atomic equation. As we enter, someone tells me not to worry, one hour of radiation here is about the same as skiing on a mountain in sunlight. I look at my watch.

ELEVEN

I drive by Port Hope every week on my commute to my teaching job in Kingston. I never stop. It's too close. I spent my teens thirty kilometres northwest of this small town on the north shore of Lake Ontario. Most summers my family would drive to the lazy shoreline, spread beach towels on the white sand and soak up the sun. My mother slathered mayonnaise onto cucumber sandwiches and watched me swim far out into the choppy water. I wanted to be Marilyn Bell, the Toronto teen who swam the lake in September 1954, thirteen months before I was born. Bell was the first to complete the crossing; she crawled out of the dark, icy water at a downtown fairground to the flash of cameras and the applause of one hundred thousand fans. I wanted to be first at something and get my picture in the paper. But more than that, I loved the fierce energy of pushing through the waves. Each stroke left something behind.

Each time I drive past Port Hope, I feel a tug. It feels silly to associate this town's part in the atomic highway with my own childhood, but that doesn't stop the butterflies that come every time I start to make a plan to stop there. I told the Dene elders I grew up beside what is now Cameco, the refinery where Great Bear's uranium was processed. It should be easy for me to check out the local archives, even visit the plant, but I keep putting it off. Finally, the weather decides for me. An early April snowstorm swings me off the highway and down the exit ramp. I park my battered grey Chevrolet outside a doughnut shop, grab a coffee and ask for directions to the Cameco offices.

Port Hope has been at the heart of a furious controversy over nuclear power for decades, a secret carefully kept from the tourist brochures. What is the connection between this place, New Mexico and Déline? How many of the chirpy kids or tired women serving doughnuts across this counter have relatives who work at the nuclear processing plant? If the grey-haired lady in the hairnet attends town meetings and environmental hearings, which side does she take? Does she support a loyal company that provides employment to hundreds of people, or does she rage at the danger of contaminated soil and water? Could the slender redhead with blossom-pink nails be a granddaughter of Penny Sanger or Pat Lawson, resident activists and author and researcher of the 1981 book *Blind Faith*? The book told the story of Eldorado Nuclear Limited (now Cameco) and Port Hope's relationship with chemical and radioactive waste.

Port Hope is an hour east of Toronto. It is easy to miss. Canada's Highway 401 consists of a dozen lanes of traffic streaming through a series of amalgamated towns: Pickering, Whitby, Ajax. The road breaks free just past the General Motors city of Oshawa. For a few deceptive minutes there are fields, farmhouses and tantalizing treelined side roads. On your left, just off the highway, the Northumberland Hills roll gently northward. On your right, factory buildings, a harbour and the Cameco sign.

I have heard several versions of how a uranium refinery came to Port Hope. The most colourful story puts Gilbert LaBine having a pint in a Toronto pub in 1931. The miner got talking to a man who owned an out-of-use pea factory. LaBine bought the place cheap over a handshake, turned it into a processing plant and hired French physicist Marcel Pochon to manage the refinery. Pochon, formerly a student of Marie and Pierre Curie in Paris, had been extracting radium from uranium at a tin mine in Cornwall, England. In 1932, he was hired to direct rebuilding and operations for LaBine. By the following year, somewhere near thirty-six tons of ore had made their way from Port Radium to Port Hope. Pochon and his team were soon producing two grams of radium a month. The sign on the highway outside town for many years read: Port Hope, the town that radiates friendliness.

The town is windy and relentlessly damp. Summer shops are closed for the season and there are no signs of swimming or summer vacations; there is nothing on the beach but abandoned running shoes and a single lonely seagull. The storm has stopped. I pass old brick and stone homes while large trees drip snow.

I stop in front of St. Mary's Elementary School. Radon gas was discovered in the school cafeteria in 1975 and the building was evacuated. The foundation had been built with low-level waste from uranium refining operations. Further investigation revealed that hundreds of buildings in the town were constructed with contaminated material; waste traces were found in the harbour, in open ravines and leaking from two dumps. The school was extensively rebuilt and reopened its doors two years later. "By then," writes Penny Sanger, "either radon gas or excessive radiation had been found in 550 Port Hope houses ... at the time of the school closing, radon gas was still unknown to most people."[58]

I stand on a bridge and stare at the nondescript buildings that house Cameco. I turn my mind to the charm of this place, which even on this grey day is evident. In another month, sailboats will fill this harbour and old men will line its banks to fish. Who wants to stir up trouble about something you can't be sure of? Then I remember Joanne Young.

Joanne was a scrappy older woman who was at every peace rally I attended in the '70s. She had married a chemical engineer who believed in his work at the Eldorado plant in Port Hope and the benefits that would come from nuclear power. One day the company was dismantling an outmoded radium lab. Ducts full of radioactive dust were pulled apart by a plumber and tossed on the floor. Bill Young was in charge of the job. He was furious about the carelessness and said so. He privately worried about how much radioactivity he had ingested. Two years later, Bill Young died of cancer. Without telling Joanne, the company took the case to the Workmen's Compensation Board and obtained papers clearing them of any connection to her husband's illness.

Joanne went on Mother's Allowance, an initiative in several provinces intended to support single mothers in difficulty or widows with dependant children. Two years later, she got a job with the local library. She wore black and opposed Eldorado any chance she got. She eventually moved away and obtained several university degrees. By the time I met her in Toronto, her children had left home and she was a full-time activist. Now, looking at the sightless windows of the Cameco plant, I wish I'd talked to her about her life. To me, idealistic and young in my politics, Joanne was an eccentric and lively presence on the picket line. I admired her but didn't think to ask her questions.

The Cameco office is right beside the lake. I ring a buzzer and am admitted into a narrow waiting room. The receptionist behind the glass tells me, "There is no library or archive at Cameco; everything is in Ottawa." If I want to meet with anyone I need an appointment. Feeling sheepish for not planning this better, I make my way to the city library and sit with a file of clippings about Blake Fitzpatrick's work with atomic photographs. Fitzpatrick is a member of the Atomic Photographers Guild and his research led to the book *Blake Fitzpatrick: Uranium Landscapes*. I flip through images of low-level waste under plastic in fields on the edge of town and glance up at this historic building, the graceful staircase; how invisible Port Hope's problems appear.

Peter has explained to me the archival path from LaBine in 1931 to Eldorado during the war to Cameco today; it gives me a massive headache. It's Kafkaesque. How does someone get access to the approximately thirty-four metres of textual documents and thousands of maps and photographs in Ottawa's files on Eldorado? Because the company was once a Crown corporation the collection came under the jurisdiction of Access to Information and Privacy. A researcher would have to know which specific document to ask for. The officer in charge would then decide – based on no clear criteria – yes or no. But the answer to the question about access is more complicated.

In 1983, Eldorado – still connected to the Crown – became a subsidiary of the Canadian Development Investment Corporation (CDIC). Five years later, Eldorado was privatized and linked to the Saskatchewan Mining Development Corporation. Together, they became what is still one of the largest uranium producers in the world, Cameco.

The government no longer had a direct link to what had been their company, so they used the CDIC to create their own corporate successor to Eldorado Mining: Canada Eldor Inc. This gave the government a mechanism to follow-up on any subsequent problems – including lawsuits. This was all happening at about the time that the Sahtú Dene were asking questions and beginning to document their land claims settlement. The creation of Canada Eldor protects Cameco from liability for anything related to Eldorado.

How does this apply to public access to information about the original Eldorado? The national archives, operating on the assumption that Cameco owned the collection, classified it "private." When they realized that the owner was actually Canada Eldor, changes were made, the collection remained closed and a request for information by the people in Déline was formally denied.

I wish I had a map to help me find Dorset Street and Marcel Pochon's famous house. When Eldorado began to thrive in the 1930s, Pochon brought his wife and daughter from Paris to live in the sleepy town. One of the few students of the Curies to live past the age of forty, Pochon hung a sign on his door: Muidar – radium spelled backwards. After the 1975 discovery of radon in the local school, the house was checked for radioactivity. I decide to save Muidar for another day.

The sun is shining. I head out of town and glance at the cars streaming by on the 401. How many of their passengers know that, for a time, this was the only uranium refining plant in North America? I told the elders in Déline that I'd grown up down the road from Port Hope. It was true, but I never knew that the town was more than a pretty place to go for ice cream. I hadn't heard this part of Canada's nuclear story when I was a high school student jumping into Lake Ontario for a summer swim and dreaming of Marilyn Bell. I hadn't even heard it when I took a bus to New York City with Joanne Young.

In 1982, the peace movement was in full swing. I was twenty-six years old and had nervously been attending peace rallies for about six months. It is three years before my trip to Nicaragua. On a summer afternoon in June, I emerge from the subway at Christie Pits, a spacious park in downtown Toronto. Dozens of people are milling about. Two yellow buses sit by the side of the park; coloured knapsacks and bags of buttons are scattered on wet grass. It has rained but the sky is blue and crisp, a warm spring evening ahead. A banner crudely painted with *Canadians for Nuclear Disarmament* is spread along the edge of the curb; a fat black Labrador pup dozes across it.

Our drive to New York City will take ten hours, most of it through darkness. There is a plan. We will arrive at dawn with what the organizers hope will be hundreds of buses from across North America. We'll unload at the outskirts of the city and board local trains into Manhattan. We'll then locate our designated places and walk to Central Park. The rally is scheduled to start at noon.

I am making myself do this. I'm not sure how I feel about demonstrations and I'm not crazy about groups, but all around me in Toronto there is a passion for fighting these weapons and I want to be part of it. I stand awkwardly on the grass wondering what bus I am supposed to get on and if it will be warmer in New York or if I should have brought a sweater. I don't know anybody; I am not part of the "scene." I've signed up for this trip as a kind of dare to myself. I need to see if I'm a committed enough person. I wonder if the black puppy is coming. That would be nice.

I recognize the Toronto Disarmament Network people holding clipboards and looking self-assured, purposeful. Committed. There's a cheerful urgency and an easy camaraderie about them. Meanwhile, I feel boring and rudderless. These activists seem so secure with each other, so caught up in the energy of the struggle, it's as if they have nothing else to worry about: meetings, demonstrations, writing leaflets, non-violence training – each day more important than the last. Rita, a practical young woman with a bullhorn, is in charge. I've seen Rita before, she shows up at every event. She gave me leaflets last fall when I went into the TDN office and asked if I could help. I spent a fun night pasting flyers onto poles along Bloor Street with a friendly American draft dodger named

Mathew. I enjoyed this time; it was quiet – no yelling crowds, no following a group, just a simple task and lots of time to talk about what was wrong with the world and what we could do about it. The sorts of conversations you have all night in your twenties.

I've officially joined the Cruise Missile Conversion Project (CMCP). Once a week, I drive with a few people to a suburb west of Toronto and hand out leaflets at Litton Industries. This factory manufactures the guidance system for the cruise missile, an unmanned aircraft piloted by a computer system and carrying a nuclear weapon. A few months earlier, Prime Minister Pierre Trudeau agreed that Canada would test nuclear weapons for the US at the Cold Lake Air Weapons Range in Alberta. Litton, a subsidiary of a California company, has received forty-eight million dollars in grants and interest-free loans from the Canadian government.

CMCP's goal is to convince Litton Industries to change what they produce into more socially useful products. We want them to use their technology to create useful navigational systems, for example for blind people, instead of nuclear weapons. This way employees won't lose their jobs when the government stops supporting the weapons. I am introduced to Joanne Young at meetings. She and another woman named Nancy Tyrell are older and make a lot of jokes. I find this both thrilling and slightly unnerving. What is there to joke about?

Sometimes there is a civil disobedience action. This is carefully prepared over a number of months. It is important to be respectful to the workers, to the police. I am both impressed and anxious about this; up to now I've only done "support." When the regulars get arrested – for lying in front of cars of workers going into the plant – I hand out leaflets explaining that we are doing this to draw attention to Canada's involvement in nuclear weapons production and testing.

CMCP is committed to non-violence. The members are thoughtful and won't accept easy answers. They also know their history. I have been reading Thomas Merton and Gandhi and find them inspiring and sobering. I realize how insignificant my life has been up to now, and how isolated. What this feels like is community, an alternative to family. Like a new set of values to put up against what I am earnestly recognizing as the selfish, materialistic way I've grown up. It's a chance to reinvent myself. That's what I tell myself, anyway. It's also what I constantly tell my parents. I will have the same reasoning when I reassure them about my trip to Nicaragua three years later.

Now, several months into my work with CMCP, determined to prove something, I'm boarding the bus. I spot an attractive guy with tousled dark hair and glasses sitting by an empty seat. I like that I don't recognize him and that he's reading a book of poetry. Daniel is older than me, in his late twenties. We cross the US border as the sun sets; guards wave us along, no inspection. Through a long, intimate night, we talk as the bus carries us steadily south. About books, about religion, about whether the world is more dangerous in the South Pacific or in Washington and how the most beautiful thing on earth is camping in the mountains. He is from New Zealand and he tells me about Greenpeace and the French nuclear tests. I tell him about the cruise missile and CMCP. We don't sleep. When we step off the bus in a New York suburb, we are greeted by a blinding sunrise and a thermos of coffee from Rita.

The vast parking lot is jammed with buses and people as far as I can see. Daniel grabs my arm and we follow our leaders down the steps into the subway. The platform is crazy; everyone seems to be headed to the same place. There are kids, dogs on leashes, students and old people with Pete Seeger T-shirts. A graffiti-splashed train car rolls into the station and we file in, signs rolled under our arms or held against our chests, lots of joking and laughing.

We climb out of the dark subway into a hot sun on Madison Avenue. I'm thrilled to be here, skyscrapers on all sides, a sense that the world is gathered in this place for one common purpose. Though I would never see him again, for a day, Daniel and I became a makeshift couple – hanging on to each other, chanting, singing songs.

The march is too big to effectively manage the different constituents from north of the border. We all blend together as one Canadian party. We stay on the street, keep moving and no matter what, we stay together. Many times I almost get lost, stopping to tie a shoelace or grabbing a drink from a vendor. But always I find Rita or Daniel and I'm okay.

I still have the issue of *Maclean's* magazine that came out a few weeks after I got back from the trip and I'm looking at it again after more than three decades. A panoramic photo stretches across the centre two pages and there among some Canadian flags, right behind the staple, is my shining twenty-six-year-old face. The child who sat at her third-floor bedroom window waiting for Richard Speck is no longer alone. The teenager who scanned the sky for nuclear missiles has found a community and a sense of purpose. Maybe it's the gloss on the paper, but I think I look happy – part of something wonderful.

When I read historical records of the 1982 New York rally, I find a woman who still believes that public protest makes a difference. Leslie Cagan has spent her life becoming an expert on the logistics of protest – how to mobilize and turn out large numbers of people, how to draw attention to a cause. Her parents were activists working for desegregation and protesting atomic weapons testing in the 1950s. She told a reporter, "It was 1968 and the world was on fire."[59] On February 15, 2003, the day Peter and I flew to New Mexico, Leslie Cagan put together a New York rally against the war in Iraq. She spent months organizing, invited Patti Smith and Bishop

Desmond Tutu and blanketed the city with flyers in a host of languages, including Arabic and Chinese. She did it again in August
2004. She was denied a permit to rally in Central Park – parks officials said the crowd would be too large. She had to remind them
about the thousands who had marched in 1982. Peter Yarrow, of
the folk group Peter, Paul and Mary, was one of the featured speakers in 2004: "This is a New York event to say: We still believe."

Those peace movement years in Toronto held a kind of innocence. But they also fomented a righteous anger. I loved it all
– loved being an activist, loved being on fire about everything.
The fury was like sugar: it gave you energy but was unhealthy. We
were fuelled by victimhood. But it was community, it was identity;
one felt lit from inside with holy purpose. Even if what we were
"against" was very clear and vehemently expressed while what we
were "for" remained significantly more vague. A friend from those
days told me, "I had *such* a good time hating these guys . . . it was
also cleansing, especially when I considered my life till then, and
my mother's life, and other women's lives. In the light of a newly
gained feminist analysis – it made me blaze and blaze for a while,
and changed everything after that."

I was on a vacation in Vancouver in 2009 when I ran into one
of my old CMCP comrades. I hadn't seen Marsha for twenty years.
"We were like a family back then," she said. After years of trying
frantically to help others, Marsha burnt out badly. For two years,
she cleaned restaurant kitchens because she had no energy to talk
to anyone. Saving the world, it seems, was not so easy. But, for a
time, some of us thought it was. I took a bus to New York City; I
was in *Maclean's* magazine. Linda Ronstadt sang.

TWELVE

Everywhere I go I meet someone with a relative or friend connected to the nuclear industry. People tell me stories. Some ask me not to reveal their identities; others hope that I will. Some say they have no right to feel affected by the atomic bomb, and that other people – downwinders exposed to radiation from nuclear testing or accidents, cancer victims – are the ones we should be worried about. I'm told this over and over. People apologize for claiming a part of this story, and then speak urgently under their breath, as if afraid to be overheard.

I meet Barry, a Japanese Canadian from Victoria, at a book reading in Vancouver. His aunt was teaching in Hiroshima the day the bomb fell. He went to Japan to ask what that could possibly have been like. The day Barry arrived, his aunt's daughter-in-law stopped by. Even though he only had one day to visit, Barry didn't think it was fair to ask a question like this when his aunt had company, so they had lunch. After the meal, he said goodbye and returned to Canada. Barry would still like to know about that day, August 6, 1945, when his aunt was a young Japanese Canadian teaching in a new elementary school.

My ninety-year-old godmother, Jenny Weir, lives in Invermere, British Columbia. She loves to tell the story of how, in 1952, when she was head of nursing at Queen's University, my parents got engaged in her living room on Barrie Street. While visiting I tell her that I'm interested in Canada and the atomic bomb, and she isn't surprised. "You had a rather explosive childhood," she says. She leans across her night table of pills and lowers her voice. "Atomic research. That was a big secret at Queen's!"

I had spent months trying to find a Queen's connection to atomic research in the 1940s with little success. Robert Oppenheimer visited Kingston on January 25, 1960, and made a speech. Jenny remembers this, but nothing was recorded and no trace remains. "There was a big party at my friend's house shortly before the end of the war," she confides. "He was head of physics. In the kitchen, some of us were whispering about the Manhattan Project. Our host was a scientist. He worked on it. He would disappear for weeks at a time and come back with a tan. While we were whispering, his wife appeared in the doorway and scolded us, 'Shhhh. We don't talk about it.' But we all knew."

Peter spends a few weeks in the summer of 2005 travelling by riverboat up the Mackenzie. One of his stops is at Tulita, "where the rivers meet," the hamlet in the Sahtú Region that we passed through on the way from Norman Wells to Déline in 2002. Tulita, forested and well south of the treeline, is located at the junction of the Great Bear and Mackenzie Rivers, and has a population of 473 predominately Sahtú Dene speaking English and Slavey. It is surrounded by mountains known for Dall sheep – Subarctic and Arctic animals with magnificent curling horns that take eight years to grow to full size. They are the only wild white sheep in the world and they are in Canada.

Peter is invited to a wedding and the entire village attends. The groom worked for Eldorado on the Great Bear River handling uranium ore. He is eighty-two years old and dying of cancer. The wedding takes place on the anniversary of the bombing of Hiroshima. Peter sends me this note, from his stop nearby at Arctic Red River:

Fourteen eagles sunning themselves at the mouth of the river. It is hot. There is an inviting pond on the large delta area at the confluence of the Red and Mackenzie rivers. High above stands the village. Walking through town, I stop and speak with an old woman who is standing near the church. I ask her about swimming in this pond. "No," she says and then tells me a long story. Following one of the innumerable battles between the Gwich'in and the Inuit, scores of Inuit were thrown into the lake, the wounded to drown, and all the bodies were left in the lake. Ever since this time, she said, the eagles wait for the bodies to rise, but all that emerge are ghosts. The lake is full of ghosts, too full, so there is just no room to swim. She uses a Slavey word to describe when this happened; I think it means a really long-ago time. Too many ghosts.[60]

In 2008, at a writing retreat in Banff, Alberta, I begin the manuscript that will become this book. I approach the lunch buffet where a fellow writer is spooning salads onto her plate. My reading the previous evening had started her thinking about when she was in university in the '70s. She saw the anti-nuclear documentary *If You Love This Planet* and remembers sitting in her dorm room with a calculator deciding if she should buy a car or donate her money to stop nuclear weapons.

I return to my room and check the weather in Déline. The Dene community is almost directly north of me and in the same time zone. It is minus three with a chance of snow, but tomorrow spring will arrive; it will be above zero in the Sahtú Region. Sunny. I turn on the television and watch a report about polar bears that wandered into Déline[61]: two cubs and an adult female lumbered down the main street, four hundred kilometres too far south in search of food. They were shot and killed. Now there is a fierce debate in the community about whether to continue shooting or try to capture and rescue. What I'm not sure about is what is being rescued: a way of life, a tourist attraction or a bear.

While I'm working on my book, other people are arriving in Banff for a Disaster Forum. One of the keynote speakers is from St. Vincent's hospital in New York, the epicentre during the aftermath of September 11. The other main speaker is talking about terrorist attacks on the London Tube. Everyone at this conference – nurses, city planners, trauma specialists – works full time in disaster preparation. I have not seen an event like this since I sought it out in my twenties in Toronto; why is it happening here, now? Disaster is no longer linked to a specific incident – nuclear war, mass murder, environmental catastrophe – it is amorphous, ubiquitous.

I start to wonder how institutionalized this fear of disaster might be. I find all sorts of Internet sites and organizations that advertise how to get disaster insurance. It looks like lots of people are afraid, and what I discover would be ludicrous if it weren't so clearly lucrative. If you pay people enough, perhaps you can keep yourself safe.

It is possible to get insurance for being stuck in bad places. The first policy I find online isn't about avalanches or tornadoes but the potential risks to international organizations "in a world of political and financial uncertainty." If evacuated under such conditions, the employee must return home within a year. The website doesn't say what happens if there is nowhere safe to return to. The information on ransom says that it is possible to be kidnapped "during your stay," making it sound like an option, along with snorkelling and shopping.[62]

I tell my fellow writers about these insurance plans as we take an evening walk along the turquoise Bow River. The snow on the mountaintops reminds me of my days in Vancouver, swimming on Wreck Beach and researching nuclear war. "Why don't you look up the survivalists?" suggests a slight woman working on a book of children's stories. "I'm from Vancouver. It's the West Coast, there must be a few of them there."

Richard Balfour, now in his sixties, is a contemporary survivalist and co-author of the book *Strategic Sustainable Planning: A Civil Defense Manual for Cultural Survival*. In 1972, he helped champion the Agricultural Land Reserve that was established to protect farmland and limit urban sprawl. Today he lives blocks from the Pacific Ocean where I bathed with my friends. Balfour helped plan the world fair Expo 86 and has organized war-game scenarios to help the Vancouver Planning Commission teach post-oil safety to the public. It's hard to write him off, and he isn't alone.

Returning home from Banff, I keep the survivalists on my radar. In 2009, a man named Paul tells a reporter that anyone not a "doomer" is a "sheeple" with her head in the sand. Sheeples "can keep munching grass." Paul was working on the eighth floor of an office tower when the twin towers in Manhattan were attacked. He went out and bought sixty metres of rope and persuaded a local outdoors supplier to teach him to rappel. He then added climbing gear to his long list of survival items.[63]

I visit my therapist one autumn afternoon in Toronto. I tell him that my writing and my life are going in circles. I don't know what I'm trying to say about this atomic story. I am hopeless at relationships with men. He asks me, "What about Peter? You trust him, you travel with him, you can be yourself with him. Isn't that a relationship?" I sit back, puzzled for a moment, then I get it. "You know what respect feels like," he continues. "And you will find what you want to say if you keep writing. But it can't be someone else's book. It has to be your book. If you don't trust that, it will never get written."

When Peter and I were in New Mexico, we sat in a Tex-Mex restaurant and sketched out a map of our travels on a napkin: Déline, Los Alamos, Port Hope, Hiroshima. We planned the book we would write together. But the events of our lives led us along separate paths. We continue to meet and talk endlessly, but we have taken different trips and written different books. Peter and his wife adopted three children and he wrote a scholarly meditation on the highway of the atom. I found a life partner, wrote an opera, bought a horse and wrote this memoir.

"I woke in bits, like all children, piecemeal over the years," wrote Annie Dillard.[64] Waking, like being witnessed, is a lifelong process. But there are moments of significance along the way. In 2004, I walked into a kitchen in downtown Toronto and met the man who would become my husband. Having a witness can change a life. My husband became my most intimate witness. He helped me mourn. He didn't provide safety – no one can do that – but he offered an alternative to my bewildering childhood. I didn't trust easily – in fact I fought like the devil. But this very good man hung on and wouldn't let go.

In the modern world, we find our way home through the work of mourning – we grieve, we face ghosts, we learn to surrender what is lost and embrace new life. This is a contemporary version of the mystics' forty days in the wilderness. The losses that mourning makes us work through are not only personal; they are tragedies that belong to our communities, our cultures. We are shaped by everything that touches us. Grief and joy bind us with the same thread. The act of mourning is a double act, intimate and public, private and political. The personal and political stories in this book are not parallel; they are inseparable.

My father's most vivid memory of the atomic bomb is of my mother coming into their kitchen with a magazine in her hands. "I was cooking, a pot was simmering, I was stirring. She just stood in the doorway, shaking, in a yellow sundress. *Life* magazine photos, I think. Thin-skinned, your mother." My father smiles and reaches a thin, spotted arm to pat me on the knee. "She was missing the tough layer, the one that keeps you safe. A strong woman on the outside. Inside, fragile. Things could break."

I'm more like my mother than I want to admit. I read all I can about environmental destruction, atomic blasts and nuclear fall-out, and in 2005, I am diagnosed with breast cancer. I receive the diagnosis on the phone while sitting in my study writing about New Mexico. I go downstairs to a bookshelf and pick up the rough bits of twisted metal I was given by Ed Grothus. It's silly, I know that these cells have taken at least five years to get into my body. Nevertheless, I wrap the rusty artifacts in silver tinfoil and shove them to the bottom of a garbage bag. I wonder where to throw it.

Navigating decisions about cancer while writing about radiation and the atomic bomb provides a certain pathetic comedy. I am lucky; my treatment is radical but brief. The experience changes me in predictable ways. I risk trusting my partner, who is steadfast in this emergency. I can't stand to waste time. Much of what worried me before stops worrying me for a good while. I take the advice of my acupuncturist about researching paradise. I actively pay attention to what is beautiful. I savagely eliminate friends who talk only about themselves. I spend more time with birds, woods and horses. I feel like a walking cliché but never mind.

I continue assembling the atomic puzzle, but am now determined to find what is life-giving in the stories and communities I encounter – their struggles, their discoveries, their hospitality. The effort to look beyond trauma is surprisingly tiring. I am rewiring myself. Mainlining tragedy is like riding a seductive current – swim against it and the resistance pulls you under. I think I have outsmarted the thing. I watch a spectacular sunset and don't think about radon gas or miner's lung. I cook supper and forget to count chemicals in my vegetables. But the habit of courting despair is tough to break, and this addiction has lots of company. Well-intentioned friends ask about my health and choke up. Confessional talk shows delight in the cruellest fate, the most vulnerable victim.

A friend visits. She tells me a story that feels like a whisper, a possible direction. French philosopher Michel Foucault traced lines of force and resistance that make up the dynamics through which we negotiate life. He reached an impasse in his understanding of power. Gilles Deleuze stood at the gate of Foucault's impasse and glimpsed something transformative. Foucault didn't only stand *against* destructive power; he stood *for* a force of life-giving vitality. Foucault was animated by the joy of wanting to destroy whatever mutilates life. In pursuit of this joy, Deleuze asked, "What if there are other lines in the diagrams of our lives? Not just lines of power or force, and more than lines of resistance?" Deleuze called these lines of flight.

THIRTEEN

Night is a memoir by Holocaust survivor Elie Wiesel that tells of a man who tries to be a witness but fails. The character Moshe lives in a village in Eastern Europe. In the 1930s, he is captured by the Nazis and taken away. He sees many other Jews murdered but he survives, finds his way home and tries to warn his community. No one listens to his warning.

There is an essay about this story. Literary scholar Ora Avni writes that it isn't that Moshe's family and friends *don't* believe him; it's that they *can't*. If they accept Moshe's story, it will disrupt the foundations of what they understand to be human. Moshe's return to his village is an attempt to reaffirm ties with the human community of his past, the very integrity of which was put into question by the incomprehensibility of what he has witnessed. But nobody can bear to hear what he has to say, or to know what he has seen. Accepting a new present would mean having to rethink everything they thought they understood about their past. Nobody wants their world to change. I think about this on the December morning in 2004, when I discover the life of Iris Chang.

The Christmas lights are up when I skim the newspaper over morning coffee. I am stopped by an unusual obituary. Iris Chang spent three years researching her 1997 bestseller *The Rape of Nanking: The Forgotten Holocaust of World War II*. She scrutinized private and government documents in four languages; toured Japan, Nanjing, Hong Kong and Taiwan; and interviewed survivors in China. Chang describes in excruciating detail mass executions and the burning alive of men, women and children – a systematic killing of three hundred thousand civilians by Japanese soldiers. It made headlines in Japanese newspapers in 1937. I put down my coffee cup. I have not thought about the Japanese as perpetrators. In fact, I don't know anything about Japan during the war except for the atomic bombs. But now, as I read on, I remember a veteran at the Atomic Missile Museum in Albuquerque saying, "We had to drop the atomic bomb. If we hadn't, thousands of Allied soldiers would have been killed, or tortured, in the South Pacific."

I find an interview with Chang from just before her book is published. The interviewer is San Francisco journalist Ami Chen Mills and the two women are at Lucy's Tea House in Mountain View, California, a few kilometres from Palo Alto. Both women are twenty-eight, and both had grandparents who had fled Nanjing before the massacre. Mills writes about her aunt, a small, shy woman, her wrists the size of napkin rings, delicate as rice paper. One day, during a heated family discussion about the bombings of Hiroshima and Nagasaki, her aunt kept quiet. Mills says, "I had pointed out to her rather talkative husband that the US government was still the only government that had dropped the atomic bomb on human beings. Hiroshima, I could maybe see, but Nagasaki too? At this point, my petite aunt spoke up. 'I think they should have bombed the whole country!' she bellowed, and then lapsed back into silence."[65]

Iris Chang was obsessed with the Japanese occupation of China prior to and during World War II. It had become embedded in her character, as if she had lived through the incident herself. She tells Mills that the Asian community wants an apology, a "guarantee that the next generation of Japanese schoolchildren will be taught the full extent of wartime atrocities committed by the Japanese. That's a good start. Right now, in Germany, it's against the law not to teach the Holocaust in public schools."[66]

Then Mills asks, "What happened in Nanjing?"

I get up from my table, go downstairs and clean the floor. Why is this so hard to read when I've been pouring through manuscripts about Hiroshima? Is it because this complicates my idea of the Japanese as victims? Because I don't want to know what terrible cost this woman paid for her commitment to, obsession with, the massacre at Nanjing? This mustn't be the only way to be a witness.

Chang spoke out against the racial profiling of Muslims after September 11, 2001. She spoke again in 2003, against the University of California for banning Chinese and Hong Kong students because of the disease known as SARS. Chang pleaded that democracy was a young and fragile experiment. Chang's friend Ignatius Ding, who financed her early research, remembers the room where the young woman wrote. It was "like a shrine," the walls plastered with documents, maps. "She would sit there and just look at all those photographs. She was like a zombie."

I turn to the newsprint in front of me. "On November 9, 2004, a thirty-six-year-old journalist died from a self-inflicted gunshot wound. She was found in her car on a side road near her home in San Jose, California. Iris Chang left behind a husband, a two-year-old son, and a number of books, including *The Rape of Nanking*."

Being a witness is an accident, an inheritance and a dangerous opportunity. The poet Jack Gilbert understood the loss and
the adventure of a life. His poem "A Brief for the Defense" includes
these words:

We must risk delight. We can do without pleasure,
but not delight. Not enjoyment. We must have
the stubbornness to accept our gladness in the ruthless
furnace of this world.[67]

Iris Chang's obituary is still pasted over my computer. I look at
the slightly yellowed photo. Her young face smiles directly at the
camera and she wears a light sweater. It is perhaps a summer day
with the slight chill of approaching evening in Silicon Valley. She
folds her arms casually but firmly, stands leaning into a faded sun
that lights up her hair. I look back at her for a long time.

In 2010, journalist Erna Paris invites me to attend a Japanese War
Crimes conference in Toronto.[68] A friend has given me *Long
Shadows: Truth, Lies and History*, Paris's account of how nations
reinvent themselves in the wake of catastrophe. The book's chap-
ter on Japan introduces me to the extent and complicated nature
of Japan's brutality. The conference is hosted by Alpha, a Toronto
organization that teaches and preserves the history of World War
II in Asia. This will be the first formal, international gathering to
listen to historians, scholars, civilians and artists tell chilling truths
about atrocities committed by the Japanese.

I arrive early on a humid Friday morning in September and sit
near the back of an auditorium in the airless university building on
Bloor Street where I was a graduate student. "The war that ended
seventy years ago is not over," says the Alpha representative. She

adjusts her jacket and gazes from the stage at several hundred people sipping coffee. I marvel at how far some of these people have
travelled – geographically but also emotionally. Around me there
are Japanese, Chinese, Canadians, Koreans, Americans – survivors
and perpetrators, all bringing a piece of a story nobody wants to
hear. Iris Chang's parents are in the audience.

Japan is still the only country to have extensively used chemical weapons. The country produced seven thousand tons between
1931 and 1945, but only three thousand tons were accounted for
at the end of the war. The rest was probably shipped to northeast
China, which was occupied by Japan in 1931. I strain to listen as
a soft-spoken professor in jeans and a white shirt says that after
1945, "unusual weapons" were seized by the US Navy and thrown
into the ocean. The Chinese didn't have the technology to dispose
of chemical weaponry, so they dumped it into rivers and buried it.

My sandwich sits uneaten in my lap as I furiously write notes,
so I won't have to feel anything as an older Japanese man relentlessly describes Unit 731. Possibly the best-kept secret of the war,
this covert and meticulously organized research facility in occupied Manchuria carried out medical experiments on human
subjects. An ambitious professor of immunology at Tokyo Army
Medical School, Shirō Ishii, headed the operation.

Ishii knew a lot of powerful people and argued for biological
warfare. Chinese slave labourers who built the compound wore
blinkers so that they wouldn't understand what they were construct-
ing. Prisoners were experimented on and kept in tiny body-size
cages, but they were fed and exercised so that their health could
provide a baseline for the testing. A ninety-six-year-old medical
doctor says that after the war, he hid near Osaka and changed his
name. He had been sent as a young man to Unit 731 not knowing
what was happening there. When this young doctor refused to kill
people, he was threatened himself, so he compromised – he would

kill only one or two a day, although sometimes the number could go as high as five.

Paris writes that the doctors and scientists of Unit 731 were chosen for their medical and research expertise. They were "neither sadists nor otherwise mentally deranged."[69] They wanted to advance their careers. When the war ended, many "became presidents of universities, deans of medical schools and heads of public-health agencies. They seem to have been ordinary men who at home during peace-time might have recoiled from causing harm, even by accident."[70]

Shirō Ishii was never charged and almost nothing about Unit 731 came out publicly at the postwar Tokyo trials. Those who ran the unit gave medical reports to the Americans in exchange for immunity. With the Cold War looming, the US wanted to make sure that the technology ended up in their hands and not with the Soviets. Ironically, it was at a Russian trial in 1949 that some medical scientists confessed, but for years the evidence was dismissed – in particular, by the American military. Paris quotes Ishii's daughter Harum from an interview with the *Japan Times* in 1982, the year Joanne Young and I attended the peace rally in New York City: "As far as I know, it is true that a deal was made. But it was the US side which approached my father, not the other way round."

On the second morning of the conference, an eighty-three-year-old Korean grandmother silences the room. Grandma Gil first spoke out in 1998. Since then she has made it her mission to tell the world how between two and four hundred thousand women and girls from all over the region – Korea, China, the Philippines, Vietnam, Thailand, Indonesia – were shipped like military supplies to service Japanese soldiers. Scholar Keith Howard writes, "It is appalling that the Japanese government, while making apologies, still maintains a stance of distance, refusing to accept that the setting up and running of military brothels was authorized by the state and insisting that a civilian fund alone be developed to pay compensation to victims. It is appalling that governments in the region, including those of Korea and China, have sought to prevent the issue coming to the surface."

In 2009, Grandma Gil spoke in Canberra, Australia. When she was finished, hundreds of Australians made online financial contributions to get the image of a butterfly and the words *Japan say sorry* displayed in the sky above Parliament House.

George MacDonell, the next person to speak, was a Canadian soldier in Hong Kong in 1941. He was taken prisoner when the Japanese army attacked the military hospital where he was a patient. The chief medical officer and his assistant were killed at the front door and every nurse was raped, murdered and disembowelled. This eighty-three-year-old grandfather calmly describes how he and the other prisoners were given twelve hundred calories a day of dirty barley and chrysanthemum tops – I scribble that they needed at least twenty-five hundred calories – and how captives were refused medical treatment. MacDonell adds softly, "Forty-six thousand Allied prisoners died in Japanese prison camps." I glance at the other side of the stage. An elderly Japanese gentleman, the other soldier who will testify today, is nodding steadily as a beautiful raven-haired young woman translates.

I think back to my trip to New Mexico. Elderly World War II veterans guided bored high school students through the atomic museum. They delivered a sanitized account of why the bomb was dropped, with no mention of the politics around Truman's decision: the opening gambits of the Cold War; pressure to show America's new weapon to the Russians and to create a test case the government could study. How do I know one of those veterans wasn't a prisoner in a Japanese camp in the Philippines?

We divide into workshop groups and I join about twenty other people in a classroom to hear former Japanese soldier Tokuro

Inokuma tell us his story. He is eighty-one-years-old, a thin man with thick eyebrows, a balding head and a gentle smile. When he volunteered for the army he was fifteen. His three older brothers had already been drafted.

"My father opposed it, but some of the first words I learned in school were 'Forward, forward, the army goes forward.'" I strain to listen to his voice and the young graduate student who is translating. Mr. Inokuma says that his training was okay, but the humiliation from older soldiers was terrible. Some recruits committed suicide. "There was one guy who jumped into a plane's propeller. But we couldn't tell his parents he committed suicide."

The young soldiers were taught that they must be willing to fight for the Great Asia, that they were superior to others of Asian ethnicity and that dying for the Emperor was the highest of honours. "Absolute obedience became our habit and preparations to kill people were always made. We were kicked in training and slapped in the face with a leather belt if anyone was too quiet or reluctant. There was no possibility of refusal. If anyone ran away, he was sent to a military tribunal and everyone told his family he was a traitor. Or, you'd commit suicide with a bayonet through your throat and chin. We were told that when the Allies captured men, they executed them, raped women, so the motivation was to protect your family."

I look at the faces around me. They are sombre, attentive and full of compassion. Mr. Inokuma begins to describe his training in the use of a bayonet. "Killing prisoners is the efficient way to get you ready for battlefield – do it early so you become strong soldiers. Bayonet is better than shooting."

I see confusion in the room; at first we aren't sure what he is saying. Then the older woman next to me gasps. Nobody is writing now. We sit together with this man who is brave enough to travel across the world and tell us how he was trained to rape women, and how he and others "tried to keep their mental balance by exploding at civilians in occupied areas."

After the war, Inokuma was captured and held for two years as a slave labourer in a camp in Sivaki, across the border from northeast China. "People held prisoner in Russia don't want to talk about their experience because they didn't help each other survive," he says.

One of Mr. Inokuma's greatest regrets is that when he finally returned home to Tokyo he learned that his father had died. It was difficult to find work. He was considered a communist because he had been freed from a Soviet camp. He changed jobs fourteen times, working as a plumber, mechanic and accountant. Now he is part of a group of soldiers in Japan who hope that Article 9 of the Constitution – the section that prevents Japan from holding an army or engaging in war – won't be revoked. We clap, thanking him, and leave the room. As I pick up my bag, I hear him speaking quietly to the translator. "It was considered the soldiers' lives were lighter than feathers."

It isn't easy for Japanese soldiers or those close to them to speak. Those who want to say anything about Japan's war crimes are called names: masochistic, non-Japanese, anti-Japanese. Reporter Tatsuzō Ishikawa was embedded near Nanjing. The writer was given a four-month prison sentence for his 1938 novel about the treatment of Chinese civilians and the pessimism of Japanese soldiers. When Shiro Azuma published *Our Nanjing Platoon,* soldiers in his regiment denied one of his most chilling accounts – Chinese tied into a mailbag that was then set on fire. Fellow soldiers sued Azuma for causing them emotional distress. In March 1998, the eighty-six-year-old author appeared before the Japanese Supreme Court to speak for his journal as a valid account of the massacre. His appeal was denied.

As these stories become public, Japanese artists respond. Iri and Toshi Maruki spent many years painting atomic bomb sufferers.

One day in the 1970s, someone in America asked them about Nanjing. Iri thought about it for a bit, then she made a mural of rape victims from the massacre. The couple went on to paint other atrocities: Auschwitz, Okinawa. Their work still tours the world. I wonder what they would say, if they were here at this conference.

I leave the building and stand outside, beside a fledgling red maple tree flourishing in its square of dry earth. I stare numbly at students hurrying into the library. I walk west through a crowd of Torontonians enjoying the end of summer on Bloor Street patios. As I reach Bathurst Street, the sky slides into what feels like a final sunset.

At a reception at Erna's home that night, I meet her guest of honour. Yoshiyuki Masaki is an ex-schoolteacher in Japan who is filing a legal document asking that the Japanese government make a formal apology for these crimes. He is gracious and welcoming, and says that when I come to Japan I must visit him. Mr. Masaki was removed from his teaching job because of his vocal criticism of Japan during the war and his activism. He says that I must come back in cherry blossom time.

I say my goodbyes and walk slowly up the hill to the subway. I turn down side streets, reluctant to leave the calm of this neighbourhood – the scent of tangled purple flowers I can't name, front porches with window boxes and inviting wicker chairs. When I descend into the train station there is nobody in sight, the only activity the frantic blink of a travel ad suspended over the platform, offering escape to the tropics.

The next morning I return to the conference. Reluctantly. I have signed up for a workshop on using art therapy with intergenerational trauma. I linger outside the room. I have spent years leading people through drama exercises yet I hate being a participant. I don't like being vulnerable and have endured too many creative arts workshops with people who don't know what they are doing. But this time I needn't have worried. Both the leaders of this short session are articulate and speak powerfully of their personal connection to Japan's wounded past. One is Aya Kasai, a slight, soft-spoken woman in her thirties from Hiroshima. Aya tells us about her two grandparents – one an atomic bomb survivor, the other a military police officer who never spoke about the war. I am moved by her quiet confidence and patient attention, and curious about this work. We speak afterwards and I tell her about the Dene in Déline and their connection to the atomic story. She says she would love to visit someday, and learn about how they are healing themselves and facing both their past and their future.

Eight months later, in August 2010, Aya sends me an email. Would I come to Kyoto to do a workshop? Would I meet her in Hiroshima? I think about this for a couple of days. Friends who know Japan say, "Don't go in December, it's freezing. Go in the spring. Cherry blossoms!" A contact in Hiroshima warns me that faculty at the universities will be getting ready for the holidays, but I am of course welcome to come and meet them. I am soon to discover that welcome is everywhere in Japan – I will have to learn how to accept it. I buy a ticket. A friend who taught English in Japan sends me instructions by email. "Above all, you must bring gifts!" So I buy packages of maple sugar from my local market and wrap them myself. My husband teases me about how homemade they look, but I'm rather proud of the folds of tissue bound in curling ribbon.

On December 14, 2010, I board an American Airlines plane for Osaka. I change planes in San Francisco. There is a slight delay so I check my email. A long note from Peter describes a family crisis. I stare blankly at passengers making themselves comfortable, crew handing out blankets. It feels wrong to be continuing this trip; I should fly back toward my friend. But the doors are closed; computers and cell phones are turned off. There is no chance to respond.

It is impossible to resist the pull of adventure when a plane takes off. I love the thrill of knowing I am about to learn something. My work has given me opportunities to meet a wide variety of people, glimpse their struggles and their triumphs. My father talked about this; he wrote documentaries and docudramas. He took his research seriously. As he plunged into worlds he knew nothing about, he honoured people's confidences and did his best to balance this with his job as a journalist and storyteller. Dad believed in the neutrality of the documentary maker. I am of a different generation. My experience shapes how I pass on stories and the kinds of stories I am drawn to. I rummage through the wreckage of history: Culloden, Munich, World War I battlefields with their unexploded ordnances. Primed and waiting, triggered to explode.

Aya's email invitation was welcoming. *I want to know your story!* But what *is* my part in this story? Apology, shame, responsibility, guilt. Who is apologizing, to whom and for what? Can there be a detective story when there is no body, no crime, no accusation?

Two poised Japanese American stewards demonstrate oxygen masks and safety gear. A third hurries down the aisle checking seat belts, bright yellow deflated life jacket over her shoulder, red whistle draped across her smart blue vest. This predictable ritual promises that American Airlines will save us – have no fear, you'll be able to stay afloat, you'll be able to call for help.

The plane begins its relentless path down the runway. Televisions are switched on and passengers start their movies. We lift over the Pacific.

FOURTEEN

I've packed too much. I wrestle my suitcase from the overhead train compartment, slip on my leather jacket and gaze out the window at the outskirts of Hiroshima. I'm cheered by the warmth of sun through glass, vibrant leaves on tree branches draped over curved rooftops. These are the last old wooden homes I'll see for a while – ahead lies a newly built, modern city. It has taken me fifty-five years to travel to the origin of my nightmares.

As the sun settles over the low blue hills, a girl about five years old, with shiny black hair and pink cheeks, flies down the aisle, arms waving. She stops abruptly by my seat and stares. Who is this tall, serious-looking foreigner? As we pull into the station, the young mother appears; laughing and bowing apologies, she tugs her daughter toward the exit. I gather my bags and follow, descending the compartment steps just as mother and child are gathered into the arms of a smiling elderly couple on the platform. The family disappears into the crowd.

The parking lot is jammed with end-of-the-day commuters filing off in all directions. I climb into a red cab with green three-leaf
clovers on the door and we head toward crowded city streets. Everything is bright lights, families on sidewalks – the Saturday night
just before a big holiday. My round-faced driver flashes a toothy
smile and shouts over his shoulder, "Everyone love Christmas in
Hiroshima. Christmas Eve big date night!"

We drive down a broad avenue that reminds me of Paris. Every
December, Hiroshima's Peace Avenue is taken up for over a kilometre with the winter festival of lights, called Dreamination:
snow palaces of light, glittering tunnels of red and silver, twinkling
horses pulling carriages, children everywhere. There are hot dog
vendors and people holding hands. We drive over several bridges,
my first glimpse of the seven rivers of Hiroshima. Everything is
sparkling and alive, nothing like the images of mushroom clouds
and agony that the word *Hiroshima* has always conjured. The taxi
turns into a narrow lane, then another, the driver consulting the
printout I gave him.

We park under a small, brightly painted sign: World Friendship
Center. I climb out of the car and offer a handful of bills, which the
driver graciously sorts. He bows, hands back my change and drives
away. I smell musty river water as I walk up a stone path lined with
a chorus of pink roses. A bucket jammed with white plastic um-
brellas waits by the door of a modest residence.

Barbara and Ron answer my ring. She is short and round, he
tall and thin. This retired couple in matching checkered shirts and
blue jeans relax me with disarming American charm, welcoming
me like a favourite relative. I think of maple syrup and pancakes,
and when breakfast comes the next morning, I'm not disappointed.
But my initial impression, that this is an American-focused house,
is wrong. The World Friendship Center was founded in 1965 to

foster understanding of Japan. It is also a place where hibakusha, atomic bomb survivors, can meet each other. Although run by a Japanese board of directors, the resident hosts are always American. "An acknowledgement for dropping the Bomb," says Ron.

Barb and Ron have volunteered to run the center for two years. They have been here eighteen months and will go home in the spring. They have spent their years since retirement looking for charitable organizations where they could be of service. Before Hiroshima, they worked and lived in a guest house for families visiting women prisoners in the mountains of West Virginia. They were shocked at the stories they heard during that time; it opened their eyes to an arbitrariness and brutality in the justice system of their own country. I am surprised by the coincidence of our interests and pull a flat parcel wrapped in yellow tissue from my shoulder bag. My gift to Ron and Barb is a calendar that chronicles the fight to save a one-hundred-year-old prison farm in my community of Kingston, Ontario.

Barb leads me up a steep, narrow flight of stairs into a bare room with a window and a thin futon on the floor, and leaves me to get settled. In what I had assumed would be a crowded city, it feels quiet. I test the futon and panic. My back won't survive a night with no support and I feel old anxieties creeping back in: *I can't stay here, I won't sleep.* I take a breath, tiptoe into the hall and call Barb. She pokes her head out from the kitchen, climbs the staircase and opens a cupboard in my room. Lined from floor to ceiling are enough mattresses to sleep ten people. She selects a particularly plump one and slides it under the futon. I grin, relieved. Barb looks at her watch and tells me I'd better hurry if I want dinner.

I find a restaurant decorated with silver Christmas lights. Through a shiny window are large platters piled with food. Young men in business suits sit at a stainless steel bar drinking beer in frosty glasses. I lower my head and duck under the black-and-white cotton banners hanging in the low doorway. A room of people look at me and all smile. A server in a red dress with a broad white sash comes forward, smiling and bowing, "Sorry, sorry, we are closed, having a party!" Even though I'm famished, I smile and bow, and apologize my way out through the printed fabric. Hiroshima, tonight at any rate, is one big party.

A branch of white blossoms hangs over the quiet riverbank and I snap a photo. The air is soft; there are purple and yellow pansies in pots along the street. A noodle house looks open, so I try my luck. I am again greeted with smiles and bows. I point to a bowl of soup on the poster of dishes, and an elderly distinguished gentleman nods and gestures to a seat. A steaming dish of shrimp, noodles and bright green vegetables is placed before me. I pick up the deep, round spoon and chopsticks and make a complete mess of it. The gentleman is immediately at my side, bows, takes the spoon and shows me how to tilt it to the side and scoop up the noodles. He laughs as I try, clumsily at first, then more successfully. He goes behind the counter and stirs another pot, smiling.

The cook stands straight; his head is almost bald. Was he living here in 1945 when the bomb fell? In *Hiroshima Notes*, Japanese postwar writer Kenzaburo Oe quotes a man who carried his father, a doctor, on his back so that the older man could help the A-bomb victims: "People in Hiroshima prefer to remain silent…They want to have their own life and death. They do not like to display their misery for use as 'data' in the movement against atomic bombs or in other political struggles."[71] What stories could this old man tell were I in the position to know him? But I am glad for the complex intricacies of Japanese society that allow him a privacy that has almost disappeared in the west.

I cross the street and sit on a bench by the river. The moon bobs like a child's toy lost in murky water. It's late, my first night in Japan;

time to sleep. But I can't move from this bench, won't surrender this moment where all I know about this country is what I have read. This is the completion of a long journey; there is nowhere to go after Hiroshima. It is the end of this story. The moon disappears, swallowed by a river that has seen too much. I wonder how the Japanese make their children feel safe. What stories are told to that little girl on the train? What helps her sleep at night?

My first sleep at the World Friendship Center in Japan is dreamless. I wake to hear birds outside my window. The toilet seat is heated. I linger and read from a book I find on the hallway shelf by Vimala Thakar, an Indian spiritual teacher. "Nothing in life is trivial. Life is whole wherever and whenever we touch it, and one moment or event is not less sacred than another."

I step into the square bathtub, slip into a sitting position with my knees bent and relax into the hot water. After a long soak, I wrap myself in a thick lilac towel and sit in my room, checking email. There is a note from a woman who is kindly introducing me to people in Japan. Junko, who I will never meet (except on Facebook), writes words that seem right out of Thakar's teachings:

No worries, Julie,
Everything I did although did not do much was but just wishing you every best in this stay nothing else.
However, the development is up to the development itself as you feel, I also feel.
Wishing you nice moments, Junko

Barb pours orange juice with a smile. "Good news!" Before leaving Canada I wrote and asked her if she knew anyone who was in Hiroshima at the time of the Dene's visit in 1998. "We are always in touch with volunteers who show people about the bomb," says Barb. "I ask one person, they ask another, you know how it goes."

This morning Barb has an email from Michiko Yamane. "She and her friend, the other volunteer, can meet you at eleven. They will give you the same tour that they gave the Dene."

As I hurry along Peace Avenue, the festive exhibits from the night before are silenced in the soft grey daylight. Traces of the previous evening's crowds have been cleaned to pristine perfection – always the way in Japan, I will discover. I approach the large gardens that mark my destination, cross the busy street and enter the modern Hiroshima Peace Memorial Museum. Two women wait by the ticket counter. Michiko Yamane's thick dark hair frames a lively face. She looks younger than me, perhaps fifty, and has been a volunteer with the World Friendship Center for a long time. "I am addicted to the place!" Michiko says.

The shorter woman with the trim lavender blouse and dark blue skirt was a very young child in 1945. Keiko Shimizu and Michiko have been taking people around this garden of memorials for over twenty years. They bow and greet me with smiles, and Michiko hands me a photocopy of a newspaper article. It is from a Hiroshima paper with no date, but it is a report of the Dene visit in August 1998. I thank her and place the clipping in my bag to read later.

We walk through the large glass doors of the museum into a bright sunny day. I am eager to ask them about the Dene delegation, but I try to be patient. I show them my new, unused audio recorder. "I hope it works!" I tell them.

Keiko takes the microphone, holds it up to her face and laughs. "I will be the reporter. Testing, one, two, three!" The birds are so noisy, when I play back the recording of the test I hear only chirping.

There are 150 monuments in Hiroshima, almost sixty in this park. We are in the centre of town but it is hard to hear the bustling traffic from the nearby boulevard. We walk first to a tree with a thin yet strong trunk and many branches rich with leaves. "This tree was half burned, it was 1.3 kilometres from the epicentre. All trees were – how do you say it, hollowed? Yes, hollowed out. People thought they were all dead, but the next spring, new shoots were found growing." Keiko speaks softly and her head tilts.

"People were encouraged by this. The new seeds were gathered and students planted them in many other countries." Keiko pulls out a small packet wrapped in clear plastic. Inside is a tiny folded paper crane, a mustard-coloured paper with a child's drawing of tiny sprouts coming from the earth and three round, wrinkled seeds that look like large peppercorns. "Aogiri. They are Aogiri seeds. I have thousands, you take!" I place the packet carefully in my bag. Within two kilometres of the epicentre, 150 trees survived, twenty varieties. Hiroshima had a campaign and many trees were sent as donations for the park. When I return to Déline in 2012, I will take the packet as a gift.

They lead me to a small plaque close to the ground. "This is a memorial for all who have died, not just on August 6, but in the years after," says Michiko. She reads aloud: *The souls who rest here will be sheltered from the elements.* We stand for a moment, then both women nod and walk on. There are a handful of tourists scattered about, one family with two small blonde children.

Michiko says that people have very different responses to this park. "I took a young army guy from America," she says. "I was telling him about all the young people, the teenagers here in 1945, they were working on munitions. I said, 'They were innocent.' He says, 'No, they weren't innocent; they were working on munitions. No innocent!'"

The sculpture of the famous young Sadako is in a small hollow surrounded by trees. It is much bigger than I imagined, perhaps thirty feet high, and on each side are small glass boxes filled with paper cranes. These origami were folded by the girl while she was ill from radiation cancer. "Sadako wanted to finish, but her dream did not come true. The writers of her story thought it was more positive, more encouragement for people, so they changed it in the book not to disappoint the children. In the book, they say she folded one thousand and then started again. But she folded maybe six hundred then died."

Aya will later tell me that the Sadako myth has a life of its own. Some say she folded up to twelve hundred cranes. "She loved to run," says Aya. "She is much stronger than she is often told to be."

Keiko approaches a middle-aged woman in a trench coat who gazes up at the statue. Keiko speaks to her, and then takes a photograph from her purse. The woman smiles, bends to look and bows to Keiko. Keiko bows back, then returns to Michiko and me. "This is my nephew, he was alive during the bombing, he died of leukaemia when he was twenty-three." She hands me the photo. It is wrapped in plastic, a faded picture of a Japanese youth in a school uniform. He is about eighteen and beautiful. I hold it for a moment, thank Keiko and return it. She looks at the photo once more then tucks it into her bag.

Keiko points across the park to the large burned-out A-Bomb Dome, probably the most familiar image of Hiroshima. "In 1967, a girl did not tell her parents, but she had leukaemia. When she was seventeen, she got very ill, went to hospital and died. Her parents found her diary. In it she wanted to make a petition to have the dome preserved. They do this. Two countries objected, can you guess?"

I don't hesitate. "The United States?"

Keiko nods. "Yes, yes. And the other? It is harder."

"China?"

She beams. "You guess good! You guess good!"

"Because of Nanjing?" I ask. Yes, yes, she nods vigorously.

"Shall we eat?" asks Michiko. "We have to meet the professor after lunch."

Professor? I have no idea what she means, but in the spirit of this trip, I will go where they take me. Keiko frowns, assessing how hungry I am. "Lunch, yes. But first, should we take you to the detonation site, the site of the blast?" I say I don't mind when we eat. The women look at each other. Michiko decides. "She can see later. Good, we have lunch!"

We cross a small bridge out of the garden into the city streets. Walking toward us is a man in his seventies wearing a funky jacket and beret. "The professor!" Keiko declares. Dr. Mitsuo Okamoto bows and we walk through narrow streets looking for our destination, an okonomiyaki restaurant decorated with plants. "I eat here all the time, it is my garden!" beams Keiko.

I am introduced to the professor's wife, who is waiting at the restaurant. Both are retired professors, still busy and active in the peace movement. We remove our shoes, climb down into a booth and sit on benches. Michiko tells me that I will now taste the famous Hiroshima omelette, the best okonomiyaki in all of Japan. It is prepared on the hot plate at the table, piping hot and steaming eggs with all kinds of fillings, cabbage and bean sprouts. When lunch is over, we cross the street to the professor's office. The dusty room is tiny with no windows and filled with books. There is one long, narrow table with many mismatched chairs. From here, he runs an organization that promotes peace. We sit down. I take out my recorder and finally ask about the Dene.

The professor is trying to remember. He asks his wife if she knows how they were first contacted about the people from northern Canada. She frowns. "Yes, Frank Cunningham! He came up behind me at the philosophy conference in Atlanta, and told me about the Dene. That was the beginning of our contact. Great Bear Lake! That's right. They wanted to come to Japan because of the uranium. They transported the uranium to somewhere in the US from Canada. This was the first we heard of it." She apologizes that she has to be somewhere else. We say our goodbyes and she is gone.

Keiko folds her hands and leans into the microphone. "It was a long time ago. We took them through the peace garden, just as we took you. They arrived late, they were exhausted and they didn't want to listen to our explanation. Too hot!" She laughs. "They wanted to go back to their hotel. Also, the hotel, not so good." It is my turn to laugh. It hadn't occurred to me until now what it would be like for a group of Dene from near the Arctic Circle to come to Hiroshima. In August! Over thirty degrees and humid. No wonder they wanted to go back to their hotel.

"How did you prepare for the visit?" I ask.

"Many people didn't prepare, the mayor didn't prepare an official meeting. It was so busy, close to the August 6 ceremonies. It happened suddenly!" When the delegation arrived, members of the Article 9 Committee – who work to keep Japan from having a standing army or nuclear weapons – rented a boat to take the Dene around Hiroshima harbour. They listened to a hibakusha story and stopped at Ninoshima, an island that was used as a refuge after the bomb fell.

The professor asks if I know why the Dene apologized. "What do you think?" I ask. "I didn't think they needed to do it," says Keiko. "Apologize. They were victims too."

The professor sighs. "Their husbands, many got irradiated, many died. It was the village of widows. The uranium was sent to the US where they built the nuclear bombs. So these people, the Dene, associated this directly with their husbands, and that's why." He gestures to the pile of newsletters on the table. "Good citizens try to make peaceful friendship. I think any such indication from the other part of the Pacific Rim would be a comfort. The US never did officially apologize, so people are thirsty for accepting."

I don't know what to make of the professor's answer. I heed the Déline chief's advice not to ask questions twice, but I am puzzled. Is the professor saying that one of the reasons the Dene apologized was so that someone would then apologize to them? Or that they were thirsty to have their apology accepted? My friend Koji, who was born in Tokyo, tells me that in Japan it is not so much to apologize – it is a question of the response. An apology accepted in Japan is a very big deal. Because it means the entire event, all its history and implication, is forgiven. The slate is wiped clean. If this is true, what happened when that Dene delegation came to Hiroshima? What is it to be implicated and take ownership in the face of a catastrophic event, and how is the response to an act of responsibility measured?

I will never fully understand the difference between a shame-based culture like Japan and the guilt-oriented culture of the West. In an individualistic society, like mine in Canada, an apology creates a sense of equity, which is usually played out through financial restitution. The Japanese – and the Dene, I think – are a communal culture, a group of interdependent selves. For them, an apology is more about restoring face, re-establishing social harmony and respect for the dead than easing interpersonal tensions.

In Japan, I hear *sumimasen* everywhere – excuse me, pardon me, I am in your way, hello. Many groups are asking the Japanese to apologize. The Japanese Labour Camp Survivors Association (JLCSA) was founded in 1989 with 6,500 people. The Burma Campaign Fellowship Group came in 1991, followed in 1994 by the Association of British Civilian Internees, with 18,300 members. All of them are asking for *shazai*, not sumimasen. Michael Cunningham writes that shazai, in the context of war crimes, is an apology for "consistently suppressing the truth about the extent of wartime atrocities," both "the initial acts" and "subsequent cover-ups." Shazai means, "I have erred for which I am truly sorry and beg forgiveness."[72]

The growing right-wing movement in Japan opposes any apology for actions during World War II. Chinese claims alone could have major implications, not only for Japan's pride but also for its pocketbook. Any opportunities immediately after the war were squandered, largely for political reasons. America, Britain and Canada wanted to maintain Japan as an ally against communism in the East and so failed to raise the issue of the Emperor's personal responsibility. The Tokyo War Crimes Trial was part of the Allies' postwar occupation plan. Rather than indicting the Emperor, the defendants were selected largely for their involvement in Pearl Harbor. Although the tribunal implemented the policy of the illegality of war, for the first time making leaders criminally responsible, they only prosecuted old political and military leaders – no one with economic or cultural power who could contribute to the west's idea of Japanese postwar recovery. Among the most disturbing omissions was the failure to prosecute any of the leaders of Unit 731.

The trial had a strong effect on the Japanese people. The Japanese were bystanders while the victors judged them. The trial covered fifteen years and was governed by Anglo-American legal principles. The evidence provoked exposure and a more massive shaming experience than any trial before or since. Those executed included General Tojo, whose failure to commit suicide when the Emperor surrendered had appalled the country, and one civilian – a civil servant named Kōki Hirota. The public opposed Hirota's sentence, and a film about him made after the war, *Tokyo Saiban* (*Tokyo Tribunal*), spent most of its time on the Hiroshima and Nagasaki bombings. After the war, the cabinet of Prime Minister Higashikuni made an appeal to the Japanese people. They called for *ichioku so-zange*, which means one hundred million representing together. The phrase absolves the leaders and accuses no one.

We leave the professor with his piles of books and papers, his phone ringing. I ask Michiko and Keiko to show me the Korean hospital where the Dene met the Korean hibakusha. Since 1945, it has been devoted to the approximately thirty thousand Korean forced labourers who were working in the city during the war. We walk around a corner and there it is, a few short blocks from the peace garden, an unremarkable building on a quiet street. Michiko takes a photo of me standing by the entrance.

"There are still Korean survivors there now, but not so many," says Keiko. "Not so many survivors left."

It is time to say goodbye. Michiko and Keiko hug me hard and thank me for coming. I watch them leave, two tiny women fading into the ordinariness of an afternoon of shoppers. I turn back toward Peace Avenue, retrace my steps through the park and watch other visitors being shown the monuments. It is a beautiful day, a fresh cool breeze, but sunny, flowers everywhere. I imagine the Dene elders walking through this memorial ground.

I sit on a marble wall running along a small pond and pull Michiko's newspaper clipping from my bag. There is a headline commemorating the Dene visit in 1998 and a few paragraphs of text. Atomic photographer Robert Del Tredici tells the story of the Dene and the uranium. Dene Elder George Blondin tells the reporter that five of his family died of cancer, including his father, an ore carrier. Keiko is "a fifty-four-year-old housewife." I fold the paper carefully, my own origami souvenir.

I am free the next day until suppertime. Before leaving Canada, I had written to tell Shaena Lambert that I loved her novel *Radiance*. She told me it was important not just to think about the atomic bomb but also to visit a beautiful and healing place. She suggested Miyajima. On my crumpled map, I find that this small island is outside the city limits. Barb and Ron are out. Meiko, a volunteer in her forties, speaks little English. I ask for directions. She searches several folders. "Wait here. I drive!"

Meiko locks the office and takes me to her small green car. I think she is driving me to a bus stop but we pass several train and bus platforms and merge onto a freeway. Perhaps she is taking me all the way to the ferry. We drive twenty minutes out of the city into a beach area of small communities and hotels surrounded by low hills. She admires my necklace. We park in a large lot beside the ferry docks and Meiko insists on paying for tickets. The ferry carries us past boats with white sails. We approach a small emerald mountain and dock near the remarkable crimson *torii*. Just as Shaena described to me in her email, this traditional Japanese gate floats above the water, a mythic and spiritual gateway to this sacred place.

The parks are filled with deer and flowers. Meiko proudly shows me the temple where the Dalai Lama recently stayed. We sit at a counter in a tiny restaurant and she instructs me to order deep-fried eel and eel (*unagi*) sushi. "Eel is a specialty everywhere here." She tells me how to say "hello" on the telephone (*moshi moshi*), and "tasty" (*oishii*), which I use immediately! I buy baked maple sweets and we ride the ferry back to the mainland. Meiko drives us to the World Friendship Center. It is almost four o'clock and she is tired. I thank her, slip my necklace into her hands and bow my way up the lane.

An hour later, back at the peace garden, I am greeted by a Jewish-American in his fifties wearing blue jeans and a windbreaker. Robert "Bo" Jacobs has recently returned from interviewing hibakusha in the Marshall Islands. He and Australian Mick Broderick are trying to connect survivors of radiation from around the world and extend the definition of hibakusha beyond Japan. We met via email through a mutual friend in Canada. Tonight, he is inviting me to a party.

Bo is in Japan on a five-year contract working for the Hiroshima Peace Institute. He likes that his salary is paid by the city of Hiroshima, even though the job is academic. I get a sense of his politics immediately. "I'm paid by the taxpayer. The budget is debated by

the city council; it's not like working for a university, which can
mean also working for a major nuclear contractor who subsidizes
the research." He strides through the graceful gardens and chats
like an old friend. Bo ran organic food stores in an earlier life but
now his field is atomic and nuclear culture. He has written several
books, and lives and breathes atomic stories. "I made my obsession
my life's work!"

On the anniversary of August 6, this park is filled with people
from all over the world. We cross the narrow arched bridge that
marks the T-shaped bomb target and Bo takes me to see the plaque
that marks the epicentre where the bomb exploded. We turn onto
a quiet street. "The small brass marker sits in front of an ordinary
house, most visitors never see it. Right here where we are standing. About a half a mile straight up." I tilt my head toward the clear
evening sky. A few birds fly over, too high up to identify.

We join people hurrying home from work and ride a packed
subway train. Bo leads me to a narrow three-storey building. I
wonder how I'll find my way home, and then realize that I will
be looked after. This is already my experience of Japan – nobody
leaves you in the lurch.

We climb a steep staircase and step into an attic room filled
with borrowed furniture. I offer a gift of maple sugar. This house is
a gathering spot for intellectuals and activists who eat, share conversation and welcome travellers. A few people prepare food in
the tiny kitchen and everyone knows each other. An intense young
man fills my bowl from an aromatic pot of udon noodles from a
stove on the table in front of the sofa. "Hiroshima isn't like Tokyo
but we have artists here," he says. "Many right here in this room!"

Aya Kasai arrives. I have not seen her since Toronto yet we greet
each other like old friends. In a few days, we will travel together
to Kyoto for her workshop. Right now she is in Hiroshima visiting
family. It is Aya's first time meeting the people in this room. Soon

she and Bo are sitting on either side of me on the couch, sharing stories about growing up with survivor parents. "I was read horrendous stories about the war and the bomb," says Aya. "Black rain, skin falling from faces, the terrible thirst. They told us, never forget!"

Bo leans across me and pours beer into Aya's glass. "In my family it was skeletons. Auschwitz. We couldn't forget if we tried. It was the same for most Jewish families I knew in America."

Aya peers into her glass, waiting for the foam to settle. "As children we were read terrifying books, shown photos, all about atom bomb victims. Last year I did a creative arts program here in Japan with people my age, third generation. I asked them, 'What kind of children's stories would you rather have heard when you were small?' Then they wrote the stories, what they wished they had been read."

Victim status in Hiroshima is a big deal. "There was a competition for being closest to the blast," says Bo. Aya nods. "Your house had to be completely flattened or you weren't really a victim, not as much as your neighbour. As for us, Jewish people are drawn to the worst trauma. It's in our blood. We know a lot about dark tourism." I ask what he means by this. "Oh, you know, people visit sites of genocide, war museums, atomic bomb blast memorials, instead of churches. Look, you and I are here. The new destination spot!"

The long flight from Canada has taken its toll and I can't keep my eyes open. Bo escorts me home as far as the peace garden. I stand in the rain and blurt out, "Why do so many people come to Hiroshima?" What I really mean is, *Why am I here?*

Bo sighs. "Maybe we're trying to understand our own childhood." He grew up in the shadow of nuclear war. In 1962, after the Cuban Missile Crisis, President Kennedy went on television and told people to build fallout shelters. This led to moral discussions about what to bring with you. "I remember an article in the

New York Times. One guy had a machine gun at the entrance to his bomb shelter. There wouldn't be many resources, and this guy was prepared to defend his family from pilferers." Our voices are loud with excitement. An old woman passing with a blue umbrella glances in mild alarm. Bo and I have some kind of shared past, a fractured history that has seeped into us, driven us to spend years of our lives working with trauma and memory, and the atomic story. Bo is the child of a Holocaust survivor. My connection to trauma is not as obvious but it is there, my own psychic inheritance.

Some early psychoanalysts thought that, without knowing it, people might "unwittingly inherit the secret psychic substance of their ancestor's lives."[73] The term *transgenerational phantom* refers to an ancestor whose suffering is transported through time, family through family, story through story. The belief that the spirits of the dead can return to haunt the living exists in all civilizations, ancient or modern. "What haunts are not the dead but the gaps left within us by the secrets of others."[74]

FIFTEEN

I am in Kyoto for Aya's creative arts workshop on intergenerational trauma. I have checked into a Japanese *ryokan*, or inn: The Three Sisters. One of the sisters, who must be close to eighty, is at the desk when I wake up. Mae is perfectly preserved, her skin translucent, her hair a large beehive fastened tightly with black chopsticks. She gives me careful directions; I am meeting Aya for lunch. I catch the Number 100 Express bus downtown and take a single seat near the back. The bus plunges into an older, busier part of town. I peer down tiny alleys at narrow wooden houses. Although Kyoto was not bombed during the war, the residents themselves burnt most of their wooden buildings to limit damage in case of firebombing.

An elegant woman carrying fresh lilies sits behind me. It is winter, but the air is warm and there are flowers in open stalls on the streets. Two teenage girls in full kimono stand in the aisle beside me, and I admire their tall white socks tucked into their sandals. The bus jolts to another halt. One of the girls giggles and grabs her friend's sparkling ebony purse. To my right, on the sidewalk across the street, a small boy confidently rides a bicycle. He is about six, his youthful mother on the bike ahead. An infant is perched in her back carriage wrapped in what looks like sheep's wool. Nobody wears a helmet. Suddenly the boy falls to the sidewalk. He shoves his left hand out to stop himself and tumbles sideways onto the curb. I wait, curious, for the mother's response. She waits for the boy. Seemingly unperturbed, he stands up, brushes himself off smartly, pulls the bike upright and climbs back on. She waves impatiently ahead and they continue on their way.

I find Aya at the appointed stop. She leads me determinedly through stalls of vegetables and hot delicacies to a small crowded restaurant. We enter, bowing and smiling, *konnichiwa*, hello, and sit at a long white counter. I marvel at the delicious smells. "May I record this?" I ask. "Yes, yes!" Aya answers. I put on the headphones and listen to the amplified clatter of dishes, the calls of the waiters mixed with melodic Japanese music. My own voice, *test*, *test*, blasts through, reminding me that I am part of this conversation, this story.

"How did you get to Nanjing?" I ask. Aya pours tea from an intricate red pot into delicate ebony cups. "My grandfather was military police in China, and my grandmother an atomic bomb survivor. So I have both sides, perpetrator and victim – I am both!"

Aya grew up with more than she could possibly handle – the silence around her grandfather's role in China and what she calls her grandmother's "heroic adventure story" of survival. "Our teachers drilled it into us, over and over, that we must never forget. The internalized message was, 'you will all die and burn up.' We were taught two things at the same time: to work for world peace and to carry a lot of hopelessness."

Aya fell in love with arts therapy. She saw a program on national television inviting survivors to draw images of their experiences and send them in. "I had always been attracted to art that comes out of suffering. I want to help people do this. Sometimes I think, I had a happy childhood, I had no suffering of my own to make those impressive great paintings, I have nothing within me that could produce this, I want to help other people do this."

She puts down her chopsticks and sighs. "I think this is my challenge. I put the suffering first and my own expression second. I am only starting to realize I, also, have trauma. Only after Nanjing did I realize. In 2007, when I went to Nanjing, I became violently sick – a lot of us did. Our bodies didn't know how to handle it."

When Aya first went to China, she thought that she and the other Japanese might be greeted with terrible anger. "I was ready to receive that, to the point where I felt so much guilt, I felt like annihilating myself. I shouldn't even exist here." This is Aya's work with creative arts therapy, to find a voice for buried grief and anger that turns physical and emotional. "We have places for dealing with physical trauma," she says. "Even environmental, but not yet for social trauma. Because the trauma happens interpersonally, intergroup, the healing has to happen that way too."

I ask Aya if it is common for people in Japan to go to therapy. "Not yet. It is still very unusual." She sighs. Then smiles. "Now I will take you, Julie, to the best place in Kyoto!"

Hosen is a famous Kyoto tea room. We enter a stone patio past tall grasses and red flowers surrounded by streams of clear water. The sun glances off the surface and for a moment I wonder what century I'm in. We remove our shoes and step up to the small seating area where tea sets and sweets are displayed. I climb awkwardly onto a square cushion. Something in this place is quiet, calm, unhurried. When delicate, gelatinous sweets arrive, I am entranced by their beauty and subtle flavours. My favourite, *warabimochi*, looks like a smoky pebble, shiny and trembling on the plate. I take a tiny bite and gasp with pleasure. Aya is pleased at my delight. This is something I notice repeatedly while I am in Japan; people go to great lengths to bring pleasure and are happy when you respond accordingly.

"The first day in Nanjing, Chinese students were talking a lot about the concrete historical facts. I think they just want to speak out to Japanese. When we learned this history, we felt a lot of emotion, for example – sadness, or weakness. A lot of Chinese were killed in the war, killed by Japanese soldiers."

At first, things didn't go smoothly. Their hosts took the Japanese visitors through the Nanjing museum and showed them evidence and testimony of the massacre. Aya and the others didn't know what to say, so they went outside and began making drawings. The Chinese passing by asked, "What are you doing?" Then the children started to draw with them. "The Chinese students in 2007, they wanted to meet more Japanese, they were so thankful that we showed up. Just showing up meant something to them. I thought, if this is what they need, we can do this."

The afternoon is almost gone. We gather our shoes; we bow our thanks. I stop in the doorway, reluctant to leave. *The Book of Tea*, written in 1906, calls the Japanese tea room "the abode of the unsymmetrical ... the purposely unfinished leaves a vacuum into which the imagination ... can pour."

We catch a bus downtown. Aya opens her laptop, hands me earphones and shows me the DVD of a project she did in San Francisco with two atomic bomb survivors. It is a form of playback theatre – the survivor tells the story, then it is re-enacted by the theatre group. "I wanted the survivors to get the experience of 'okay, they heard me!' In Hiroshima, they are almost professional storytellers. One woman told us that when she speaks to a large audience of schoolchildren, she always takes a sedative, a sleeping pill, before telling the story."

Sometimes the creative arts therapy work Aya studies focuses on the pain of life and doesn't take into account the importance, even the existence, of joy. She once designed a poster for a play-back performance and tried very hard to make the image beautiful. The director of the performance thought the artwork made the show look frivolous. I am struck by the calm confidence of this young woman, and her bravery. She is determined to be in her own skin and live her own life. I had barely glimpsed this kind of self-awareness when I was in my thirties. I wanted to save the world but I failed to see its beauty. This strikes me now as odd. What was it I wanted to save?

I am nervous as we head to the workshop. It is not just that I will be speaking; it is the creative therapy that Aya will lead us in later. I have no idea, as we take the elevator to the sixth floor of Ritsumeikan University, that it is my own secrets I am about to encounter.

We find a small classroom crowded with chairs and tables, a lectern and fifteen people in animated conversation. Aya introduces me. Her colleague Kuniko Muramoto is a clinical psychologist who works with women and children survivors of domestic violence and abuse. When she gets to the bottom of these situations, she often finds war veterans who were violent at home. This is what took her to China. Kuniko is interested in the children of perpetrators of mass violence. There are few studies on the children of Nazis, despite the psychology boom of the '60s and '70s. And while interest in psychology came much later to Japan than Germany the issues are the same. "What happened to our own generationally transmitted perpetrator trauma?" Kuniko asks. "I can't help relate this to problems today with Japanese youth. There is an epidemic of wrist-cutting and overdose."

Kuniko and Aya went to China together, and Kuniko has written about what that first trip meant to her:

My mother is a survivor of Tokyo air raids and I grew up listening to her stories of hardship. When looking back, I too protected myself by saying, "War is in the past and it has nothing to do with me"; drawing a line between myself and my mother's incomprehensibly horrific stories, so that I would not get overwhelmed and fall apart . . . When the right time came, I opened my heart and went to Nanjing. It is hard to describe what came as a result, but whatever "it" is, it is a very good thing.[75]

Tonight's session is part of a monthly symposium where participants use creative arts – painting, drama, sculpting – to understand how trauma is passed from generation to generation. Some of the people here are young and many have families who were devastated by the war; one or two were children in 1945. They all want to understand their connection to Japan's complicated history. Not everyone has support for this. When one of the graduate students told her parents she was going to Nanjing with Japanese young people, they said, "Why do you go there?" Her father said, "That is past. It is too heavy for you and it is not helpful for your job, your career."

As I wait for the workshop to start, I wonder what these people will make of Canada's part in the atomic bomb. I have a flash of anxiety similar to my experience in Déline, but it is different now. I seem to be over my liberal guilt and can no longer draw tidy lines between witnesses and survivors, victims and perpetrators. More and more these stories seem to involve all of us.

I talk to the group about my work with communities who have made plays from difficult situations. I read from Brecht's poem "To Those Born Later":

What kind of times are these, when
A talk about trees is almost a crime
    Because it implies silence about so many horrors?[76]

I say that art is both impossible and necessary. Aya helps a young man translate. He seems puzzled by how I phrase things. The two consult, turn to me and repeat with smiles, "So poetic!" I get through about a quarter of what I'd planned. I didn't realize how much time and energy it takes to translate.

Aya takes over. She asks us to stand up. Even though I work in theatre, I hate "touchy-feely" exercises. As much as I like Aya, I am uneasy. We introduce ourselves and say something about what connects us to World War II. Then Aya divides us into groups of three. Each person in the small group is asked to make one physical gesture that indicates how the war still lives in his or her family or life. Emiko, a middle-aged woman in my group, begins her gesture. She covers her ears and tells us that there were many secrets in her family. It seems a simple enough thing to say, but she becomes emotional and holds her hands tightly against her head. She looks from me to the young man standing beside her, drops her hands, stamps her foot and says, "I ask questions and they get angry!"

It is my turn. I feel awkward. I am the only white person in the room. This is a good thing to experience. Floundering, not sure if I have anything important to contribute, I step forward with my left foot. I lean toward my two partners and my left hand reaches for them while my right hand stretches out behind me. "This is me, always wanting to learn about this war, but, at the same time, not wanting to intrude on people." They watch me with no expression. The position is hard to maintain and Emiko laughs, grabs my left hand and pulls me toward her.

We are all given a large sheet of thick paper and told we can take anything from the pile in the middle of the room. Aya has assembled magazine articles, markers, scissors – it looks like a kindergarten classroom only there are no cookies. Everyone gets to work while I stand around awkwardly. I drift to the magazines and am drawn to a few images: ice breaking in the spring, a figure in a snowsuit ice fishing alone, a small cabin in the mountains buried in snow, a nurse standing in a crowded emergency room. I check to see if anyone is watching, pick up the bits of paper and take them to an unoccupied corner of the room. I sit on the floor, paste the images onto the paper and am overcome by feeling. I, like some of the others in this room, grew up surrounded by secrecy – everything covered up or buried, nothing said out loud. As I build my image, it becomes hard to breathe. I know what I would tell this group, what image I would make, if they asked. But I'll never let them ask.

I tear a bit of text from one of the newspapers: *History is vague.* I paste this right in the middle of the collage, then start ripping edges off each image and stabbing holes with a pen. Then I remember the dream.

I watch the murders on our black-and-white television. I become obsessed with how the one nurse who survived, Corazon Amurao, had escaped notice. I need to know how to do what she had done. I sit awake at my bedroom window, keeping watch. I wait for the man who will turn into our yard, enter our house. While my brother and parents sleep, I keep watch.

At first it's hard, but it gets easier. You pull a chair to the window, lean your elbows on the ledge, poke a two-fingered slice in the curtains and you watch. Your attic bedroom is thick with summer heat. You want to open the window but a crack would be too much. A crack could be opened from the outside. The street is shiny from a steady rain and drops hang onto the big maple outside. You think about Hayley Mills climbing out her window in that Disney movie, *Pollyanna*, named after a girl who is endlessly good natured and optimistic. You don't care about that; you know you'll never be Pollyanna, but you would like to have the adventures she has. And then you notice how close the branches in your tree are to your window and you think, "It's as easy to climb in as to climb out."

You know you'd be harder to spot in the dark. There are lots of ways to be invisible. You count on your fingers how many ways there are to disappear. Hold your breath. Keep still. Hide under the bed. No, he'll be smart about the bed; he won't be fooled that way again. Maybe the closet. Turn out the light. Pretend to be someone else. Run. Fly away.

He's out there. You smell him, as surely as he smells you. He's damp and sweaty, his breath minty, his fingernails tiny, perfect curves. One by one they slide into my skin. He wraps his arms around my waist, breathes my soap. I'm washed from the bath, fresh new pyjamas, soft flannelette. He nuzzles the curve of my shoulder, slides into my black curls. I stay down, knees on the floor. I hold my breath and switch off the lamp. A great dark swallows the room. My eyes adjust. I adjust. I adjust.

The girl from the dream doesn't like what she's thinking. She likes the standoff, the high pitch in her blood, the hot closeness of his hands – or the thought of his hands, all that man's attention eating her up. Like she's the sweetness at the bottom of things. Like she's the most important thing he's ever laid eyes on. She gets to decide, in this contest between them. If she'll feel him or not – if she'll let him really be there, in the house, in her room, in her mind and on her skin. Or if she won't. And that's what she loves most of all – that suspended moment that stretches and stretches, that's all hers and all hers. And then she decides.

She says to herself, "Your thoughts come out a certain way, but you can make them go where you want." She decides to change what she thinks. She tries it. Making her thoughts do what she wants.

I see a crack of light under the door.

Footsteps.

My mother coughs, the toilet flushes.

I imagine her leaving the bathroom.

She opens the door.

She picks me up, snuggles me.

I'm brave enough to tell her. "He's coming." She nods. She knows.

"We'll stop him," she says, lighting a cigarette. "We'll trick him."

"First," she takes a puff, "we'll change the number on our house. What number would you like to live at?"

I think. What's the right answer? She's waiting for me. Can I say whatever I want? "Thirteen!" It's a guess. I look at her face. I can never tell what she thinks.

She smiles. "That's good." She pats my arm. "You're my smart girl. The elevator never stops at thirteen."

I know my mum has more to say, more ways to confuse him, more ideas. I know if she keeps talking he won't find our house. She'll sit on my bed and tuck me under the thin blanket. I'll fall asleep smelling her musky cigarette and perfume, and I won't even need to dream because she'll keep watch.

And now that I've changed what I think, the man goes away. Puff, in a puff of smoke. And the room settles down and behaves itself.

Sometime in my mid thirties, I woke from a nightmare and couldn't stop screaming. My boyfriend took me to the hospital and a nurse finally got it out of me. What had come back, through the dream, was the memory of weekends I had spent between the ages of two and five in my grandparents' house. A few days later, I called my mother and told her what I'd remembered. She listened, hung up the phone and a few minutes later called me back. She said that my father would talk to me. It had been his father who had done things to me when I was little. The grandfather who I had put out of my mind for thirty years. The grandfather who gave me a typewriter when I was sixteen because he knew I wanted to write. I never took it out of its case.

My father met me the next day at the Swiss Chalet near Yonge and Dundas in Toronto. He sat down, ordered his dinner and was so nervous he dropped his fork. I loved him for that. "Yes," he told me, "what you remember happened."

At age five I had refused to get into the car with my grandfather. Later that day, I told my mother why. She then told my father, who immediately drove to his parents' house in a rage. He confronted his father in the kitchen and yelled, "You will never see my daughter again!" My grandfather rushed from the room, my father left the house and my grandmother stood there looking bewildered. It was never explained to her why I was never allowed to visit again.

I didn't remember any of this until I was thirty-five and even then I didn't understand why I thought the world was so unsafe. Now, in this classroom in Kyoto, I sit looking at my collage of frozen ice and torn images. Suddenly, I laugh and paste the emergency nurse right in the middle of the collage. That's me, trying to save the world! I glance at Emiko, working carefully on her drawing. I am glad I will show her my picture without having to explain.

Joseph Wolpe, one of the founders of behavioural therapy, studied animals that were very afraid. Wolpe is best known for something called "systematic desensitization." This involves "imaginary exposure to a feared stimulus while at the same time applying relaxation." Do animals behave like us? The metaphors for being revealed are not surprising: they found me out, I was exposed, I had nowhere to hide.

Before we leave, Aya gives us each a small ball of clay. "Please make something that says what you are taking away from this workshop." It is clumsy and simple. I expect to be embarrassed, but instead I am moved. In just a few months, Aya will return to Japan to volunteer near the Fukushima nuclear plant. Perhaps she is onto something, this simple, vulnerable communication – this willingness to be honest. I don't know.

We conclude the evening at a brightly lit Chinese restaurant. Everyone is laughing and chatting. I sit at a small table with three of the men. The translator has spent many years taking Japanese students to China. He knew Iris Chang. "Yes, he worked with her," Aya tells me later. "But he burnt out. He was taking it on."

The second gentleman works with families of men who were forced labourers during the war. The waitress brings plates piled high with noodles while he tells me how there were shortages in the ports and mining towns of Japan, and between 1943 and 1945, almost forty thousand Chinese were abducted. Before being sent to Japan, Chinese farmers were kidnapped and put in concentration camps, then sent "as cargo on ships. If they died, they were thrown into the sea, gone." He pours a spicy red sauce onto his plate and keeps talking.

Landing in Japan, they were stripped of clothes and made to wade through pools of antiseptic water. The man talks on, excitedly. I want him to stop. "If man wouldn't put his head under he is hit. Then taken out of the pool, not given a towel, has to put on still wet clothes and is given a number. Not controlled by names, numbers. They were kept in cracked wooden huts, no heat, straw on the ground. Men would embrace each other in sleep to stay warm, often wake up to find companion dead. Mouldy rice and bran powder to eat, bits of stones, bits of vegetables, ten hours of work, no break. If they had to work in the mines, they were often naked, somebody tries to stand up, the overseer threw an axe head and broke his leg."

My face must look terrible because suddenly he stops talking, shakes his head. "Sorry, sorry. You didn't know this? Sorry." I tell him that all I learned about Japan in school was the atomic bomb. "Same in Japan, that's all people taught," he says.

An hour later, I'm in a cab speeding through downtown Kyoto, accompanied by one of the workshop participants. Mr. Nakagawa teaches here but we discover that we did graduate work in Toronto at the same time. My companion teaches Indian philosophy and holistic education: "A very odd mix," he laughs. "No problem in Toronto, there are many open minds and ideas come from every-where. Here in Japan, I don't know enough because I'm not an In-dian scholar. Everything is very rigid and precise, and can't deviate from the expected." Mr. Nakagawa wrote his thesis about Indian thinkers and is still trying to do work on enlightenment. We agree on this; enlightenment would be a good idea.

I wave him off in the cab and step into an oasis of calm. Three Sisters Inn is at the end of a short curved pathway through tropi-cal plants and past a small waterfall. The air is warm and sweet, and everything is lush. At the front desk, Mae tells me she has sent everyone away on holiday because they will soon be busy with Christmas. I am the only guest. My room is quiet and peaceful. A futon with fresh white sheets and an elegant duvet sits in the middle of the floor beside a small heater. At the back are two arm-chairs and a low table; through the large back window is a garden with a goldfish pond.

I climb into my pre-warmed bed. On the sliding doors are deli-cate fans painted in silver and blue. Despite everything that has happened tonight, I feel at peace. As I fall into a deep sleep, I re-member something Aya said. After the party in Hiroshima, she looked around at the crowded streets of people celebrating the hol-iday season and sighed. "We grew up, we children are alive, why doesn't anyone see that as hopeful? Like we don't exist? My city is not only about bombs!"

The next morning, I roll my suitcase through the Kyoto Sta-tion. The high glass ceiling of this magnificent building crowns a glorious forty-foot-tall Christmas tree. A large poster advertising the musical *Evita* looms over a train attendant who smiles, bows and ushers me through the gate. I walk up the platform to the line that indicates my car number. When the flashing silver bullet train curves in, I am in exactly the right spot and the doors open at precisely 10:34 a.m. I find my seat with the commuters and stow my bags underneath. I have one more appointment in Hiroshima. I sit back and take a breath. My trip is almost over.

SIXTEEN

Walter Bayha wants to see the parliament buildings. This Sahtú Dene elder and former chief has been to Ottawa before, but always there are meetings. In June 2013, I find Walter and Deb Simmons eating with friends at the Sweetgrass Aboriginal Bistro. Bayha has a broad, friendly face, greying black hair and a quiet manner. I ask him what people in Déline are thinking about Port Radium today. "Learning that history, it was about healing. The young people needed to know, how come their grandfather died? How come these things happened? Some of the old people went back over there to the mine, brought the young ones with them. They needed to do all that."

The man with the glasses sitting across from me was the Chief Federal Negotiator for the Sahtú Land Claims Settlement. Kevan Floor worked in Déline for six years until the agreement was signed. I ask Floor about the Dene's report *They Never Told Us These Things*. He frowns. He isn't so sure about some of what was in it but he understands why it was written. Then he tells me about the boat.

"Everybody was afraid of the *Radium Gilbert*. They thought that the showers were bad. That was ancient history, you could sleep on that boat for a hundred years and never get any radiation!" Floor knew that the community wanted the old tugboat gone. It was too painful a symbol of the past, sitting out there in plain view for people to look at every day. Deb pipes up, "It was the first place I took everyone on the tour of Déline."

The government, prompted by Floor, agreed to remove it. The process took years and cost a fortune. Why? Because the boat, long rid of radiation, was covered in lead paint. "The whole thing was so toxic, special platforms had to be built so that when they sanded off the paint, it didn't end up in the lake."

At a goodbye party for a colleague at Queen's, I met Doctor Richard D'Aeth, an elderly gentleman, who had practiced medicine in the north. He had visited Déline and was part of early land rights negotiations. I asked him about the health of the place. Did he think that the uranium has done lasting damage? "When you were there, did you think it was safe for the Dene to eat the caribou, to drink water from Great Bear Lake?" I asked. "I don't know about that," he replied, "but I can tell you one thing: they shouldn't eat so much Kentucky Fried Chicken."

There are always more sides to a story. And more secrets. One rainy night in 2000, a man walking his dog in Massachusetts found a suitcase full of black-and-white photographs. He lived in Watertown, home during the postwar years to a military arsenal used for ballistics testing and nuclear research. The photographs were curled, dirty and bent, and revealed devastated buildings, twisted girders, broken bridges and panoramas of a destroyed city. The man – Don Levy, co-owner of the Deluxe Town Diner – put the photos in storage. Years later, he mentioned them to a customer who helped him contact a New York gallery. The photos were exhibited in 2003, but the show was largely ignored.

Then reporter Adam Levy looked into the story. Don and Adam Levy (no relation) attempted to locate the owner of the house where the pictures were found. They tracked down a local phone number. The voice on the other end, Mark Levitt, sounded shocked: "The photographs? Of Hiroshima? You have them? I thought they were in my basement!"[77] Levitt got the pictures from a friend, who found them in a house where he worked as a painter. The photos were taken as part of a Physical Damage Division assembled by President Truman to quantify the effects of the two bombs.

The Japanese government suppressed information in numerous ways following the dropping of the atomic bombs. In September 1945, Australian Wilfred Burchett visited a partly destroyed hospital and described, "patients dying, mysteriously and horribly – people who were uninjured in the cataclysm – from an unknown something which I can only describe as the atomic plague."[78] Burchett couldn't convince any official to carry the story to Tokyo, but he managed to get it to a colleague who circumvented the censorship office. The article appeared on September 5, 1945, in London's *Daily Express*.

When Burchett returned to Tokyo from Hiroshima, he arrived in time to confront General Leslie Groves at a War Department press conference. Groves, the man in charge of the Manhattan Project, told the press that Japanese deaths from radiation were due to poor Japanese medical care. The Australian journalist had another version of events. He had seen a stream on the outskirts of Hiroshima where fish would swim a little distance then turn belly-up and die. A few days after the press conference, Wilfred Burchett was admitted to hospital. When he was released, his camera with the footage from Hiroshima had mysteriously disappeared, and there was a command from General MacArthur ordering Burchett to leave Japan immediately.

It wasn't only the Americans and the west that kept secrets. For ten years after 1945, there was so little public discussion in Japan that the *Chugoku Shimbun*, Hiroshima's major newspaper, had no movable type for the words *atomic bomb* or *radioactivity*.

Paul Tibbets's first job in a plane was dropping Baby Ruth candy bars over a grandstand of people during a Florida horse race. Tibbets was interviewed by journalist Bob Greene when he was eighty-three years old and still writing with an elegant hand. In the early 1970s, the man who piloted the atomic bomb to Hiroshima ran a corporate jet-for-hire service in central Ohio and drove a Toyota. "I see so many aggressive drivers. It is much more nerve-racking for me on the freeways of Columbus than it was flying the *Enola Gay* to Hiroshima."[79]

In 1998, the year the Dene flew to Japan, Tibbets told Greene, "I try to do things right." The two men's conversations were recorded in Greene's book *Duty: A Father, His Son, And the Man Who Won the War*, published six years before Tibbets's death in 2007. The pilot was put in charge of the atomic bomb mission when he was twenty-nine. He oversaw the work of eighteen hundred people in Wendover, Utah. Greene is trying to understand his own father, also a pilot, and over the course of several meetings, Tibbets opens up with the younger man:

> I am an orderly man. When I stay in a hotel room, I fold up the towels. I usually make the bed before I leave ... I don't like the idea of other people doing something that I can do myself. A sense of order is very important to me ...
> ... At twenty-nine, I was so shot in the ass with confidence ... *I didn't have anyone who I had to ask what I had to do.* I just did it.[80]

After the war, President Truman invited Tibbets to visit the Oval Office, offered him a cup of coffee and asked if anyone gave him a hard time about what he had done. "Yes, sometimes that happens."

"You tell them that if they have anything to say, they should call me," said Truman. "I'm the one who sent you."

Three months after my return from Japan, I watch television reports of the crisis in Fukushima. Three months after that, a fire in Los Alamos forces the evacuation of eleven thousand people from the city and there are concerns that thousands of outdoor drums of plutonium-contaminated waste will overheat and burst. In December 2011, World War II veteran George MacDonell, the man I'd heard speak on a stage at the Toronto conference on Japanese war crimes, is on the front page of the *Globe and Mail*. Seventy years after MacDonell was taken prisoner in Hong Kong, Japan has made a formal apology to Canadian prisoners of war.[81] In December 2015, the Japanese Prime Minister formally apologizes to Korean "comfort women" and the government provides a fund of over eight million dollars for survivors. The government does not admit legal responsibility for what happened.

One of the most curious developments in this story is the shutdown of the Waste Isolation Pilot Plant in New Mexico. The world's first permanent underground disposal facility was meant to continue operations until somewhere around 2039 and then be sealed shut. I receive an email from Peter in 2014 telling me that one of the waste drums – Number 68660 – experienced a "violent exothermic reaction." This means that it exploded and contaminated the underground facility.

On February 14, radiation detectors on the surface picked up readings of plutonium and americium, which are specific isotopes "that could be traced to the waste interred six hundred metres below. Panic. Lockdown...WIPP is now shuttered for the foresee-able future."

Peter tells me there are a number of theories about what caused the explosion, but the thinking is that "the kitty litter – yes, kitty litter – that is routinely used to stabilize nitrates in radioactive ma-terial (basically stopping it from drying out and getting way too hot) had been replaced with organic kitty litter." While normal kitty litter, made with bentonite, acts as a stabilizer, organic kitty litter, made with wheat, in this context acted as fuel. It produced the makings of a bomb.[82]

The Déline Uranium Team (DUT) has spent years researching the effects of the mine on the community. In 1998, they sent a del-egation to Ottawa. A year later, the DUT agreed to a co-operative process with the federal government to research the health and environmental impacts of the mine. The resulting Canada-Déline Uranium Table (CDUT) Final Report was released in 2005 and made twenty-six recommendations. Some have been addressed and clean-up work, in partnership with the Dene, is ongoing. But the report also concluded that there was not enough evidence to link working for Eldorado to cancers in the area.

The CDUT report has faced criticism both inside and outside Déline. Environmental journalist Andrew Nikiforuk expressed concern that the narrow framing of the study weakened its find-ings. Intertek, the official fact-finder hired for the CDUT, was not able to access key archival information. The only statistics con-sidered relevant in the determination of cancer-related deaths are body counts. But cancer researchers argue that using death records to assess the effects of uranium on a population is insufficient.[83]

The Dene report also mentions the Japanese: "We are suffering intense guilt and grief in our community that the materials we carried to the barges and to the aircraft went to make an atomic bomb that killed many tens of thousands of human beings in Japan. Our people feel that if they had been told what they were helping to do, they would not have done it."[84]

The Hiroshima Peace Museum is almost deserted. Down a narrow hallway is a small seminar room. A thin elderly man in a silver-grey pinstriped suit is talking to ten or twelve people. Mr. N. holds a pointer and, like the school principal he was for many years, taps a map of Hiroshima. "Two lines go north and streetcar goes this way and Hiroshima harbour is north. US air forces succeeded to hit rear centre of the city. They did a good job. Almost 80 or 90 percent destroyed in a moment. Still they say Hiroshima-type bomb is a small one. Small one? Unbelievable. Okay."

I am embarrassed to be late and slip into a seat halfway back. I turn on my tape recorder, hoping it will work. Later, I ask Mr. N. if it is all right that I recorded his talk. "Of course!" he says. "This is why I do it."

My mother died the year before I learned about the uranium mine at Port Radium. My father, almost ninety and lonely, gives me a box of his notebooks – ideas for radio and television scripts interspersed with diary entries about our family. I find a note he made about my mother on April 24, 1961: *Sandra wants to drive to Florida because there is no future.* My father wrote this just days after the failed CIA-sponsored attempt to invade Cuba, The Bay of Pigs.

August 6, 1945, was a Monday. Just before takeoff, flight surgeon Don Young handed pilot Paul Tibbets a small cardboard box containing twelve cyanide capsules, one for each member of the team – in case of an emergency landing and possible capture. Tibbets later said that if the mission had failed, he would have been court-martialled and sent to prison. "Nobody knew I existed. No one knew our unit existed."

The *Enola Gay* started to taxi at 2:37 a.m. The runway was a thin path through jungle and the bomb was heavy. According to Tibbets, "some of the crew on the flight were getting very nervous as I kept the plane on the runway so long as we were taking off. There was a cliff-like drop at the end of the runway, and some of them were thinking about that ... I needed every inch."

Mr. N. speaks lightly and punctuates his points with soft laughs. He is now eighty-one. I quickly calculate that at the time of the bombing he was fifteen. Or sixteen.

"My middle school days full of long war. And as you know, the situation became worse and worse for Japan. We began to lose everywhere. So. 1944. One year before the end, situation was very bad. Shortage of all kinds of material, you know, very poor. Food was problem of course. We were hungry. We students were mobilized to work in the factories, no school. Yeah, imagine! No school! Work, hungry, terrible days. Yeah."

The plane took off from Tinian Island's North Field at 2:45 a.m. with Little Boy tucked safely in place. There were small explosions along the runway from the flashes of photographers who'd been alerted that something big was breaking. One of the crew thought it was like the opening of a Broadway play. When the plane was underway, navigating by stars above and barrier reefs below, Tibbets crawled through a twenty-six-inch circular tunnel to tell the men at the back of the plane, "This is what it's all about."

The target was the T-shaped Aioi Bridge in the centre of the city. When they reached the spot, Tibbets thinks he said, "Do we all agree that this is Hiroshima?"

Mr. N. had been working in a factory – there had been no classes – but at the beginning of August the students had been told to come for some brief schooling. So they went. He raps on the board.

"Fortunately our school had started at eight o'clock in the morning. So we were already here. You see, if our school had started at 8:30 or nine o'clock like these days, we must have been in the centre of the city and maybe burned and killed in the streetcars. Maybe barbequed. Ha! How lucky we were. At eight o'clock, the first period, math class, had already started and we were in the classrooms. Yeah. Very lucky. Okay."

Bombardier Tom Ferebee released the *Enola Gay*'s bundle at 9:15 a.m., approximately five hundred fifty metres over the city. Navigator Theodore "Dutch" Van Kirk wrote in the plane's log, "Bomb away." Physicist J. Robert Oppenheimer had told Tibbets to turn 149 degrees as fast as he could, then to get the hell out of there. The rolling shock waves tasted like lead. Tibbets smoked all the way back to Tinian. He told Bob Greene over fifty years later, "Nobody told me not to."

At 2:58 p.m., the plane landed back on Tinian. Tibbets was decorated with the Distinguished Service Cross, while the other members of his crew received Air Medals. On August 9, 1945, the *Enola Gay* flew reconnaissance to Kokura as a support plane for Special Bombing Mission Number 16, which dropped Fat Man onto the city of Nagasaki.

Mr. N. invites questions. Most of the people listening have travelled here from America. They are solemn and respectful. Someone asks why his English is so good. He loves this question and responds with glee that he ended up teaching English as a foreign language to junior high students. His favourite city in America is Boston but he has visited relatives who live in Hawaii. "I visited Honolulu, very funny, they took me around the island but they didn't take me to Pearl Harbor. Why not?" He couldn't ask because of the war. "They must have had very complicated feelings to us. That's why he didn't take me. So I didn't ask. If I could visit next time again, I will!"

Mr. N. wants to visit the memorial of the USS *Arizona*, a tomb to the 1,177 soldiers killed when the ship was bombed during the surprise attack by Japan on December 7, 1941. "I want to pray the spirits rest in peace. American soldiers, American victims. They were the victims of the war. Anyway. Very funny story, isn't it? Another complicated, yeah ... very difficult experience to me." At the end of the talk, I thank him. I say that I am from Canada and that uranium for the bomb came from my country. "I should apologize," I say. He doesn't hesitate. "That's okay," he says.

Hiroshima has more bars than anywhere in Japan, most of them in this district. Aya locates a small door with a tilted sign. We show our tickets and walk inside a dark room with a bar. A young man slips from behind a velvet curtain and sits at a piano. He plays a jazzy classical number. Everyone is standing but I am the oldest person in the place and Aya notices. She points to a spot across the room. We squeeze through the crowd and hop up onto some metal cabinets.

A young woman in a pale shift with traditional white *butoh* makeup on her face takes the stage. The music plays and the dancer begins, performing the almost imperceptible movements that characterize this art form. I have seen butoh only once, years ago in Vancouver. Then I was bored and impatient, but this performance is different. Or perhaps I am different. Tonight I hang on every shift in the woman's pose. As she holds her arms forward, hands dropped in front of her, I stifle a gasp. This dance replicates precisely what I saw at the Hiroshima Peace Museum: a lifelike sculpture of a woman lost in the white ash of August 6, arms reaching forward, searching for what? Home? Loved ones? The familiar life extinguished in a fraction of a second? When it is over, I clap, filled with emotion for this emotionless art form that I now see with new eyes. "She has come all the way from Kitakyushu," Aya whispers. "There is no butoh in Hiroshima."

The headliner from Tokyo enters. A statuesque woman with wavy black hair, she is costumed in dark silk stockings, red garters and a simple black and crimson bodice. While she tests the ropes hanging from the ceiling, a small band of young men tune instruments. They begin a pulsing rock rhythm; the stripper twists her body in slow, delicious seduction. She grabs the rope with both hands, gives it a short tug and leaps into the air, wrapping her legs around the winding cord and dropping her head backwards.

I watch the audience as she removes revealing bits of clothing. There is a combination of lightheartedness and tension. "Don't be embarrassed," whispers the dancer. She offers a sisterly smile to a group of men near the front who stare intently at their drinks and refuse to look. There is a comfortable laughter in the room. I laugh too, feeling shy, aroused and curious at the same time.

The band is terrific, the performer first-rate, but eventually Aya and I tire and, reluctantly, we leave. Aya helps me buy a bottle of sake for my husband and we go our separate ways. On my last morning in Japan, I pass the noodle restaurant where I spent the first evening and cross Peace Boulevard in the bright sun. Three tiny elderly women sit on the bench eating cherries and talking. I catch a streetcar from the bridge by the World Friendship Center and enjoy the competence of mastering public transportation. The next stop is announced over the automatic loudspeaker – Atomic Dome! The Peace Museum slides past on my right; a group of young men in suits wait by the entrance.

I hear "Jingle Bells" blaring through a loudspeaker in front of the covered arcade of shops. I buy gifts for my family and friends, then take the streetcar back to say goodbye to Barb and Ron. A cab takes me to the train. We drive along Peace Avenue and I take one last look at the light display of pirate ships and princesses, sad

and ordinary in this cloudy afternoon. At the station, I grab a delicious oyster soup and board the high speed *Shinkansen* for Osaka.
We arrive at Kansai International Airport just before five p.m.; the
setting sun is in my eyes. It is December 23. At home, people are
doing their last-minute shopping and my husband is preparing to
pick me up at the airport. I buy boxes of exquisitely wrapped chest-
nut sweets at the airport, savour a last real Japanese sushi meal and
catch a plane for San Francisco.

I sleep most of the way and wake to leathery eggs mixed with
sour brown strips. I already miss the elegance and beauty of Japanese dishes. Passengers shove one another, trying to get to the
washroom. Courtesy takes a different shape in North America. But
good manners don't necessarily mean good health. I remember
men in downtown Hiroshima wearing impeccable business suits and
teetering drunk as their friends push them into a cab. *Salarymen*.

I've barely noticed the middle-aged woman with fair hair at
the other end of my row. As our plane approaches San Francisco,
she asks me what I was doing in Japan. I prepare myself for the
usual response – surprise and admiration – as I tell her about the
Dene, the mine and the apology. "A lot of the uranium came from
Canada," I say sombrely. She smiles. "Oh, well. If you're looking to
attract guilt."

I look at her more closely and notice the books in her shoulder
bag, the intelligence in her eyes. This is a new reaction to my narrative. Is it true, am I looking to attract guilt? I tell her about Aya and
how she takes young Japanese to China. "Oh, yeah," the woman
replies wearily.

"What?"

"Lots of students go to China and Korea. Korea is the top travel
holiday destination, China probably second. They get their face
rubbed in it, there's a lot of 'you did this to us.' For some of them,
even their grandparents weren't alive in the Second World War."

I ask why she thinks the Japanese are so friendly with Americans. Bo Jacobs told me that after the war, the country had to choose between being occupied by the Soviets or the US. "They are glad to be with America, that's why they are affluent and not in the position of Eastern Europe." According to Bo, there is an undertone of resentful obedience among many Japanese that finds its way into business and political relationships with America. "Japan playing the obedient child to the American parent, not allowed to have its own foreign policy or army, not allowed to act like any other nation." This is why the rising influence of the right wing is pressing Japan to rearm. "Last fall, the mayor of Nagasaki was killed for speaking out about Japan's war crimes history and his work for peace." Perhaps this is also what underlies Japan's insistence on being a nuclear power.

I get none of this from my fellow passenger. Her name is Alison, and she has lived and taught university in Japan for twenty years. "Japan is a forward-thinking country," she says. "So is America. Native people, slavery, it's not my fault. It's a long time ago."

Clearly there is more of a conversation to be had, but we have landed. I ask if I can interview her. Alison has a connecting flight to Albuquerque. We look at the departure screens – there isn't time. I find my usual Air Canada gate and wait for the boarding announcement. I arrive at the front of the line but they won't let me through. I have forgotten that I am flying United and have missed my plane.

I stand in the help line with frantic passengers trying to get home for Christmas. Seven hours later, I catch another flight and arrive in Toronto on the morning of the 24th. My husband is waiting for me. I chatter all the way to Kingston, then completely lose my voice and lie on the couch while he goes out for Christmas dinner with friends. It takes two days for me to be able to say a word. I'm completely content.

A month after my trip, I email Alison. She doesn't answer.

SEVENTEEN

Peter van Wyck and I are guests of the Writers Read program at Concordia University in Montreal and have just finished reading from our atomic manuscripts. A young man in a dark blue shirt approaches my chair. "I'm doing a Ph.D. in poetry," he says, "but I spend half of the year up north in Yellowknife. Of all the small communities in the north, Déline is the most vibrant, the most vital. So much is happening there. It's fabulous!"

Michael Nardone crosses in front of our table to speak with Peter. Back in 2002 I visited Déline as a disaster tourist. I saw nothing but trauma and death, my anxiety leaking through. By the time I got to Japan that anxiety had lifted. In Hiroshima, I saw the effects of trauma, but also a thriving place full of life. Hiroshima is still alive and so am I. Perhaps it is time for one more trip.

I fly to Déline on August 6, 2013, the anniversary of the bombing. The timing is an accident – that's when I can get a flight. I have spent weeks trying to link my visit to the annual Déline Spiritual Gathering, where people from all over the area come to honour the prophet Ayah and share his teachings. I can't get anyone in Déline to confirm the dates and so finally I book something. I then find out that, to my dismay, the Spiritual Gathering will start the day after I leave.

I retrace my steps from eleven years ago: Edmonton, Yellow-knife, Norman Wells, Tulita, Déline. Libby Gunn, a Parks Canada worker, kindly offers me a spare room. When I fly in, Libby is away on a fishing trip with Morris Modeste. At the airport, I recognize a stylish woman in a dark jacket. She offers me a ride into town. Nine years ago, Irene Bayha worked with the Uranium Team. Now she runs the Grey Goose Lodge.

I drop my things at Libby's and go for a walk. The shoreline is bursting with life: statuesque fireweed waving mare's tail, tiny flowers I can't identify. Great Bear Lake sparkles and the crisp air is a welcome relief from the humidity of Eastern Ontario. I visit the cemetery, high on the hill overlooking the water. I was wrong to remember tiny white crosses; the graves are surrounded by rectangular picket fences of baby blue, green and yellow. There are bouquets of plastic flowers, a feeling of gaiety.

I follow the path along the shore. As I stoop to take a photo of the blazing pink fireweed, a slim teenager in a ball cap emerges from the brush. "Did you just move in?" he asks shyly. "Just visiting," I reply. I stop by a dock and dangle my feet in the water. It isn't as cold as I expected. I could almost imagine swimming, but not quite. I pass the boy again on my way up to the main road. "Did you get good pictures?" he asks me. This time he grins. Old friends.

The grocery store is closed so I go to the Grey Goose for dinner. The lodge is smaller and cozier than I remember. The restaurant is sold out of fish and chips so I buy a surprisingly good cheese-burger. As I leave I notice the large stuffed polar bear, the same unfortunate female I'd seen on TV while I was in Banff. Later I am warned by an elder never to go out into the bush, or even around

town, without a gun. Bears are dangerous. So is the water. "Never
go in a sailboat, it'll kill you." Every family here has lost someone
to drowning.

I unpack and browse Libby's bookshelves. If I had lived another
life, this could be my house; our aesthetic taste is identical: reds
and blues, beautiful objects combined with just a little clutter. The
silence, the birds, the air. The city so very far away.

Two days later, Libby arrives with armfuls of camping equipment and her friend Nikki. Over dinner they tell me stories. My
favourite is of a local wedding. It's twenty below and the guests and
wedding party had waited for ages outside the church, the young
bridesmaids in red silk, strapless dresses, Libby in her parka. She
had just arrived in Déline. On the flight from Norman Wells, she
had shared the plane with a prisoner in handcuffs and a huge box
that the pilot placed carefully on the floor. It was a wedding cake,
large enough for a double wedding. "Please don't step on it," the
pilot had asked Libby and the prisoner.

My week passes quickly. Outside the community centre some
of the elders, the women, tan caribou hide and teach anyone who
wants to learn. I stop by several times and have a go at handling
the tough skin. A very old woman in a purple sweater with a bright
blue scarf tied around a cloud of grey hair skilfully scrapes gristle
and blood from the skin with a sharp blade. I fumble to hold the
knife and awkwardly pull down along the amber hide. I am exhausted and have to quit after just five minutes. My teacher rewards
me with a plate of hot bannock, flour and water cooked on oil over
the fire.

I am invited to talk about my work on Déline radio. This is the
best way to reach everyone who is not out of town, on the lake or
in the bush. Many of the elders listen to the broadcast every day in
their homes. Ruby Beyonnie will translate for me. She shakes my
hand and I sit beside her at a table covered in sound equipment.

Ruby is my age with smooth skin like a girl. She switches on the microphone and introduces me in Slavey.

I say that I travelled to Hiroshima and met the two women who guided the Dene delegation in 1998. "They showed me a tree with a strong trunk and many branches rich with leaves." Ruby smiles. "The tree was 1.3 kilometres away when the bomb exploded. It was burned, the trunk was hollowed out and people thought it was dead. Next spring, new shoots grew. People were encouraged by this. The new seeds were gathered and young people planted them in many countries."

I tell them about the small memorial in Peace Memorial Park with the engraving, "The souls who rest here will be sheltered from the elements." I read an email I received from Keiko just this morning from Hiroshima, sending her good wishes. I tell them what the apology meant to Professor Okamato. Then I talk about my first visit to Déline. "I was lucky enough to visit Peter and Theresa Baton; they welcomed me to their home and talked about the uranium mine." Ruby gasps, switches off the microphone and covers her face in her hands. "They were my parents!" she murmurs through tears. "You met my parents! My parents!" I grab her hand and we sit there quietly. She sighs, takes a deep breath and switches the microphone back on.

The wind blows down Great Bear Lake. The bow of the boat slices a steady line through silver waves. Deb Simmons huddles in the bow facing into the wind, wrapped in a down jacket and yellow slicker. At the engine behind me is her partner, Morris Modeste, dark eyes on a horizon as familiar to him as breathing. It is a sunny morning; warm enough for a light jacket on shore, below freezing out here on the water. Great Bear Lake, where my book finishes and Peter's begins: "Mile zero of the Highway of the Atom, where the wind blows with a fierce intensity, falling down the ancient hills, pouring onto the lake to lift the water's surface into waves."[85]

Morris's flat metal boat bounces over the water heading northeast along a shoreline dotted with small white spruce. Ahead, kilometres across the water, is the old mine site. I wonder if I'll ever come back here, perhaps make the trip that Peter and I had talked about sharing. I'd told him I get seasick and would rather stay onshore. Today I'm not so sure.

Morris casts a fishing line into the water. The wind has dropped and the sun feels hot on my face. The water quietly laps against the side of the boat. Deb dozes, her head nodding onto her chest. A gull floats overhead. This morning, while Morris loaded the boat, Deb joked with three small girls throwing pebbles into the water. They are the next generation in this place. Like the child in my opera, they are about the future. I remember the old Dene man at the meetings years ago, when Peter and I first spoke about the highway of the atom: "If you have something in your pocket, pull it out, otherwise it will rot." The rod bends sharply and Morris pulls in a large glistening grayling. He tucks it into the net and drops it on the floor of the boat. Then there is another, and another. "Enough," he says. "Time for tea."

It never really gets dark here in August. Libby draws the curtains but even my sleep mask doesn't help. At four a.m. I try to read. There is a faint star in the sky. I think I liked it better in the winter, as strange as that sounds. With constant light there is no privacy. "Too much light and too much dark," a woman at the grocery store tells me the next morning. "It's challenging to be a white person living in the north. You'd find out if you stuck around. There's one woman, she's lived here years, married a Dene and made a good life. But for most of us, you're always from away." This is a perspective on Déline that didn't occur to me the last time I was here. "The chief says it's important to bring people up from the south and allow them to work with the community," she says. "Not chew them up and spit them out." Smart man, I think.

Libby takes me out of town in her jeep, and we climb dry hills and pick raspberries on a ridge overlooking the broad lake. Déline nestles against the shoreline, a thin dark ribbon occasionally catching the light. I scratch my hand on a bush and photograph orange berries surrounded by vibrant purple leaves. An hour later, there is a rare sighting of muskox on this same plateau; it's the talk of the town. We missed it.

After supper, I walk along the wooden sidewalk through dusty streets to a last visit with Morris and Deb. Morris has an old log cabin right at the edge of town. Deb offers me homemade molasses cookies and a jar of shampoo she made with local soopolallie berries. I set up my laptop and play them music from the opera. *Shelter* is a fable about a nuclear family and a couple who give birth to a glowing girl who is the atomic age. Hope, the sixteen-year-old daughter who symbolizes the new world her parents can't control, sings her desperation to blast out of her little town. Morris and Deb listen attentively. I look out at the lake through their large window. The spot where the prophet Ayah had his vision is a few kilometres away.

Morris tells me he has frozen the grayling from our fishing trip and I can take it home to Kingston on the plane. The fish is almost three feet long. Two days later, when I unwrap the green garbage bag in my kitchen, the fish won't fit into any of our pans. We cut it up, share it with neighbours and I throw the guts into Lake Ontario to feed the gulls.

On my last day I finally meet the new chief. He is young and well liked. "I didn't seek out the job but I'm doing my best," he tells me in the Band Council office. He asks why I'm not staying for the Spiritual Gathering. "That would be the best way to understand this place." I explain that I couldn't find out the dates in time and had to book flights before they got even more expensive. "Aren't you willing to spend your own money, aren't you a professor?" he asks. I am taken aback at his bluntness. "I am in a drama department. The arts, not a hotbed of funding," I say.

I return to his office that afternoon and a receptionist points toward a room where a group of men and one woman sit talking at a table. I enter and stand for a moment. No one looks at me. Then the chief says, "This is Julie Salverson, she has come from Ontario and she can't stay for the Spiritual Gathering. Doesn't want to spend her own money!" He laughs. I wonder if I don't understand his humour or if he is being deliberately rude. The assumption here is that anyone coming from the south has infinite resources from the cash cow that is the government or – if they are hunters or fishermen – their own deep pockets. I am tired of hearing about what white southerners are like. "If I'm not supposed to presume I know who you are," I think, "why do you have the right to presume you know me? There is a wretched history of colonialism and inequality, but my personal finances are none of your business."

I am surprised to find myself thinking this. Eleven years ago, I wouldn't have had the capacity to be angry. I wouldn't have been able to take anyone in Déline down from the pedestal of my own white guilt.

I spot a chair in the adjoining office, carry it in and set it at the table with the Band Council. I say I am extremely happy to be in Déline, and to see all the initiatives underway and how beautiful it is here. I say I was grateful for the opportunity to speak on the radio. I say that the premiere production of *Shelter* will happen shortly, and that the opera company in Edmonton wants to invite two people from Déline to attend. One of the men asks me about Port Hope. He seems interested and I remember speaking with him at the caribou workshop the day before. He tells me that the Dene are a kind of chosen people, and that when the world faces a global disaster, the only place with clean water and food will be Great Bear Lake. I heard this story from several people during my visit.

When I finish speaking, the woman looks at me. "We don't like it when people take our stories and profit from them. We ask for some of the money." She is talking about the opera. I look back at her. The whole history of my people and hers sits between us in this moment. What role am I being asked to assume in this endless drama of exploitation and ignorance? What role is she assigning herself? Suddenly I don't want to play anymore. I refuse the terms. I want to answer honestly, for myself, and that seems both an enormous effort and the simplest thing I can do.

"This is not your story," I say to the woman. Then I look at the men. "This is my story. What I have written and what we are doing is inspired by what has happened here in your community. The composer and I think it is important that people know about that and it is our intention to tell them. Is that all right with you?" The woman is the only person at the table looking at me. "All right," she says.

On my first trip to Déline, I went ice fishing. Gordon Taniton, his round face framing a flashing smile, teased that I didn't have "northern patience." I climbed aboard his red skidoo and we followed the shoreline of Great Bear past tiny houses puffing smoke; the sun bled fire along an indigo horizon. We lurched onto the lake and headed full steam toward a small white canvas tent over a kilometre out. Gordon switched off the engine and the silence roared back like a giant wave hitting an empty beach. He took me inside and proudly showed me a battered couch and an airtight stove. He loaded it up with wood, tossed in a match and pointed at a dark circle cut out of the floor. "The fish down there aren't just food. They give us Sahtú people our freedom. Maybe one will find you."

He handed me a cold black rod. "Don't let the fire go out – you'll freeze! Sit yourself on that couch, prop your feet to hold you steady and drop your line down. Then wait."

The snowmobile disappeared into the dusk. I pulled out my copy of *They Never Told Us These Things*. The bundle of papers fell open to a page I hadn't noticed before – a map, drawn in pencil, of the mine on Great Bear Lake. Small squares indicate locations of interest: the tugboat that carried the ore, a tennis court (beside chemical bags), houses for miners (beside sewage dumped in the water), a bank, store, skating rink, school. In a small circle is written, "deep pond on top of hill." Outside the circle: "child drowns, pond drained."

The map – situated as it is inside a report sent to Ottawa, a book on a shelf, an archive – shows what French historian Pierre Nora calls *lieux de memoire*. These are sites where an intersection of history, memory and engagement blocks the work of forgetting and carries with it a will to remember; they are transitive moments in the culture of a living people. Running diagonally across the map are two long, narrow strips, with a row of tiny arrows inside each. These are the underground tunnels that lead from the mine to "way far" under the lake.

Great Bear is a beautiful spot to sit and fish. I think of the 740,000 tons of radioactive tailings left in the lake beneath me. Thorium-230, a hazardous nuclide found in uranium tailings, has a half-life of about eighty thousand years. What is the half-life of memory?

"I am, you are, by cowardice or courage, the one who finds a way back to a scene," writes Adrienne Rich. The act of returning is part of the work of mourning. The work of mourning takes us home. But how do we mourn when there are too many dead? The site of loss is no longer the bomb site or the burial ground but the planet. There is nothing new in the country of grief.

How far does catastrophe bleed? We live in a world from which there is no escape. It is the only home to which we can return, bloody and brilliant. What is there to do but muster the courage to feel our own emergency, take responsibility for it and ask what it means to how we live? We are overwhelmed by so much but we settle for so little. We desperately need each other and there is no road map. Because life is brutal is it then futile? Can we imagine a future that acknowledges the past but isn't shackled to it, that reaches toward us as we risk a greeting?

In the living room at the World Friendship Center, in a book of Buddhist stories, there is a tale of a tiny boat caught in angry seas. Only one person in the boat remains calm, doesn't panic. If you can find the courage and the integrity to be yourself, if you are your best self – calm, lucid and aware – then you will be what is needed for the situation to improve. The story ends: "I wish you good luck. Please be yourself. Please be that person."[86]

As I have followed this highway of the atom, I have excavated the architecture that shaped me. It is easy to think that the scars that mark us are nothing beside the ravages of history. But the distance between is a hair's breadth. For years I insisted that the two paths I followed were separate – the route of Canada's uranium and my story of witnessing the wondrous and the wounded. Now, I see them as one.

At the height of a summer evening, I stand in my kitchen and look at my voluptuous garden. A pale yellow rose is trying to open. The neighbour's fat grey cat waits to catch a songbird. I want to chase her away but tell myself, I'll never know the garden's beauty if I don't enter its darkness. I pour a glass of wine.

ACKNOWLEDGEMENTS

I owe an enormous debt to the Banff Centre for Arts and Creativity and my mentors there: Myrna Kostash, Edna Alford, Marilyn Bowering, Stephen Galloway, Isabel Huggan, Ian Brown, Katherine Ashenburg and, above all, Don Gillmor. Thanks to my fellow writers at the 2008 Writing with Style, 2009 Writing Studio and 2010 Literary Journalism programs; much of Banff's magic is due to you.

Sections of this book first appeared in *Maisonneuve* magazine ("They Never Told Us These Things," 2011, Honorable Mention National Magazine Awards) and the anthology *Theatres of Affect* ("The Secrets of Others," 2014), and I thank Drew Nelles and Erin Hurley for their editing of those pieces. "The Babysitter and Me" was a finalist for the CBC 2009 Creative Nonfiction Literary Award. Excerpts from this book were part of an essay that received honourable mention (with Peter van Wyck) in the *Malahat Review*'s Creative Nonfiction Contest, 2008.

I received funding support from several institutions and I owe them great thanks: the Toronto Arts Council, the Ontario Arts Council, administrator Helen Floros and publishers Cormorant, Biblioasis, *Brick: A Literary Journal* and Wolsak and Wynn. I thank the Canada Council for helping me get to Japan and Queen's University's Fund for the Support of Artists on Faculty for getting me back to Déline. The Social Science and Humanities Research Council of Canada generously funded the early work Peter and I did and made possible our trips to Déline and New Mexico. Queen's

University's Department of Drama and my terrific colleagues there supported me in taking time to work on this manuscript.

I had some amazing editors along the way: Craille Maguire Gillies, Mady Schutzman, Don Gillmor and Susan Olding read early drafts with thoroughness and insight, and told me things I needed to hear. Other readers helped me understand what I had found and needed to keep seeking: Lynn Fels, Mary Rose Donnelly, Ruth Howard, Bobby Lucy, Chris Wells, Patricia Fraser, Carolyn Smart, Nancy MacMillan, Diana Wyatt and Kate Sykes. Friends offered ideas and support along the way, in particular I thank Stacey Curtis for telling me there needed to be resting spots from the tough material, Steven Heighton for the Japan conversations, Barbara Hannigan for her atomic stories, and Juliet Palmer and Wayne Strongman for the years creating our opera *Shelter* that indirectly fed this book. Thanks Raelene Young and James Price for writing time in your Pembroke home, John O'Brian for atomic inspiration and Lawrence Ballon for being an eloquent witness.

I want to thank some of the kind and generous people who opened doors and answered emails along the way. In Déline: Deborah Simmons, Theresa and Peter Baton, Walter Bayha, Orlena Modeste, Rita Baton, Morris Modeste, Libby Gunn, Allison Rew, Gina Bayha, Danny Gaudet, Gordon Taniton, Ruby Beyonnie and the elders and community members who made me welcome. In Japan: Ron, Barbara and Meiko at the World Friendship Center, Robert Jacobs and Carol Agrimson, Junko, Keiko Shimizu, Michiko Yamane, Dr. Mitsuo Okamoto and his wife, and Eri Nakamura. In New Mexico: Scott Zeman and my kind hosts in Alamogordo. Thank you, Peter Blow, for the film that started it all.

Noelle Allen and her team at Wolsak and Wynn are amazing. Noelle sent me a handwritten note in 2008 when she received ten early pages, and asked me to send her the manuscript when it was ready. Her belief in this book over the years has meant the world.

No writer could have a stronger or more tireless champion or more insightful editor. Thanks to Andrew Wilmot and Ashley Hisson for copy-editing brilliance, Joe Stacey for publicity support and Marijke Friesen for the gorgeous cover.

This book has been shaped by many good souls, not all of them human. I would never have gotten through a summer of writing about Japanese war crimes without horses. Thank you to Morag and Selena O'Hanlon and all the great hearts at O'Hanlon Eventing and Balsam Hall in Kingston. Most particularly, thank you for finding me Henry.

Aya Kasai invited me to Japan and shared with me her remarkable insight and intelligence. I am grateful to have found a friend who insists on the spirit of beauty in the face of the unspeakable.

Peter van Wyck was with me from the beginning. *Merci.*

Vera de Jong has guided this book with her friendship, her editorial eye and her ability to put words to so much of the experiences we shared as young activists and women. Vera, this book would not exist without you.

Bill Penner has been editor, bullshit detector, hand holder and friend. Thank you for your patience during the years of my preoccupation, my time away from home and my anxiety. Thank you for reading multiple drafts and always telling me the truth.

Some names not mentioned here, or mentioned only briefly, are given more time in the bibliographic essay. To all who I have forgotten, my deepest apologies. And my thanks.

NOTES

1 David Adam, "The Day the Sky Exploded," *Guardian*, July 31, 2003, https://www.theguardian.com/science/2003/jul/31/science.research.

2 Robert Jay Lifton and Greg Mitchell, *Hiroshima in America: Fifty Years of Denial* (New York: Grosset Putnam, 1995), 345.

3 Spencer Weart, "Nuclear Fear," in *Filling the Hole in the Nuclear Future: Arts and Popular Culture Respond to the Bomb*, ed. Robert Jacobs (Lanham, MD: Lexington Books, 2010), 245.

4 Loudon Wainwright, "The Nine Nurses," *Life*, July 29, 1966, 18–27.

5 Ibid., 21.

6 Ibid., 26.

7 Teresa Simm, "Visits from the Other World: The Operation of Transgenerational Haunting within the Process of Japanese Performance Creation" (graduate paper, University of Toronto, 1995), 10.

8 Simm, "Visits from the Other World."

9 George Blondin, *When the World was New: Stories of the Sahtú Dene* (Yellowknife: Outcrop, 1990): 78–79.

10 Déline Dene Band Uranium Committee, *They Never Told Us These Things: A Record and Analysis of the Deadly and Continuing Impacts of Radium and Uranium Mining on the Sahtú Dene of Great Bear Lake* (Déline: Dene First Nation of Deline [*Sahtúgot'ine*], 1998).

11 Cindy Kenny-Gilday, "A Village of Widows," in *Peace, Justice and Freedom: Human Rights Challenges for the New Millennium*, ed. Gurcharan S. Bhatia, J.S. O'Neill, Gerald L. Gall and Patrick D. Bendin (Edmonton: University of Alberta Press, 2000), 116.

12 Quoted in Peter C. van Wyck, *The Highway of the Atom* (Montreal: McGill-Queen's University Press, 2010), 23.

13 Ngũgĩ wa Thiong'o, *Decolonising the Mind: The Politics of Language in African Literature* (Westlands, Nairobi: East African Educational Publishers, 1986), 17.

14 Ibid., 22.

15 Linda Griffiths and Maria Campbell, *The Book of Jessica: A Theatrical Transformation* (Toronto: Coach House Press, 1989), 35.

16 Rosemary Jolly, *Cultured Violence: Narrative, Social Suffering, and Engendering Human Rights in Contemporary South Africa* (Liverpool: Liverpool University Press, 2010), 114.

17 Ibid., 115.

18 Rudy Wiebe, *Playing Dead: A Contemplation Concerning the Arctic* (Edmonton: NeWest Press, 2003), 119.

19 Frederick B. Watt, *Great Bear: A Journey Remembered* (Yellowknife: Outcrop, 1980), 210.

20 Ibid., 41.

21 Ibid., 104–5.

22 Fred "Tiny" Peet, diary entry, 1980, NWT Archives, Prince of Wales Northern Heritage Centre.

23 Michael Polanyi, *The Tacit Dimension* (Chicago: University of Chicago Press, 1967), 4.

24 Joy Parr, *Sensing Changes: Technologies, Environments, and the Everyday, 1953–2003* (Vancouver: University of British Columbia Press, 2010), 7.

25 Ibid., 8.

26 Peter C. van Wyck, "Community Talk" (unpublished manuscript, February 2003), Word file.

27 Ibid.

28 Ibid.

29 Quoted in Jolly, 98.

30 Kelly Oliver, *Witnessing: Beyond Recognition* (Minneapolis: University of Minnesota Press, 2001), 17.

31 Van Wyck, *The Highway of the Atom*, 126.

32 Ibid., 127.

33 Quoted in Wiebe, 135.

34 Wiebe, 134.

35 Gloria Galloway, "Reserve Brings Humans, Nature Together," *Globe and Mail*, August 11, 2016.

36 Boris Cyrulnik, *The Whispering of Ghosts: Trauma and Resilience*, trans. Susan Fairfield (New York: Other Press, 2010), 40.

37 Ibid., 41.

38 Ibid., 13.

39 Ibid., 130.

40 Wiebe, 99–100.

41 Ibid., 101.

42 "Scientists back Navajos fighting uranium mining," *Indian Country Today*, March 12, 2004, http://indiancountrytodaymedianetwork.com/2004/03/12/scientists-back-navajos-fighting-uranium-mining-90083.

43 David Lowry, "Ed Grothus," *Guardian*, March 24, 2009, https://www.theguardian.com/world/2009/mar/24/ed-grothus-obituary-nuclear-weapons.

44 Shoshana Felman, "Education and Crisis, Or the Vicissitudes of Teaching," in *Testimony: Crises of Witnessing in Literature, Psychoanalysis, and History*, ed. Shoshana Felman and Dori Laub (New York: Routledge, 1992), 5.

45 Debra Rosenthal, *At the Heart of the Bomb: The Dangerous Allure of Weapons Work* (Reading, MA: Addison-Wesley, 1990), 23.

46 Hugh Gusterson, "The Legacy of Ed Grothus and the Black Hole," *Bulletin of Atomic Scientists*, December 18, 2008, http://thebulletin.org/legacy-ed-grothus-and-black-hole.

47 Nicolas Abraham and Maria Torok, *The Shell and the Kernel*, trans. Nicholas T. Rand (Chicago: University of Chicago Press, 1994), 122.

48 Anna Mehler Paperny, "The Search for a Nuclear Graveyard," *Globe and Mail*, August 25, 2009, last updated August 23, 2012, http://www.theglobeandmail.com/news/national/the-search-for-a-nuclear-graveyard/article4288430/?page=all.

49 Quoted in Gordon Edwards, "Canada and the Bomb: Past and Future,"

Canadian Coalition for Nuclear Responsibility, June 1996, http://www.ccnr.org/opinion_ge.html.

50 Quoted in Edwards.

51 Robert Jungk, *Brighter Than a Thousand Suns: A Personal History of the Atomic Scientists*, trans. James Cleugh (New York: Harcourt, Brace and Company, 1958), 188.

52 This letter was discovered by Peter's research assistant, Sandra Gabriele, in Library and Archives Canada.

53 Tim Lilburn, "How to be Here?" in *Living in the World As If It Were Home* (Toronto: Cormorant Books, 1999), 19.

54 Ibid., 18.

55 "Science: Atomic Footprint," *Time* magazine, September 17, 1945.

56 Quoted in Lifton and Mitchell, 31.

57 Ibid., 72.

58 Penny Sanger, *Blind Faith: The Nuclear Industry in One Small Town* (Toronto: McGraw-Hill Ryerson, 1981), 61–62.

59 Laura Longhine, "Behind the Protest: A Lifelong Organizer," *National Catholic Reporter*, March 14, 2003, http://www.thefreelibrary.com/Behind+the+protest%3A+a+lifelong+organizer.+(Behind+the+News).-a099019890.

60 Peter van Wyck, "Field Note: Tsiigehtchic (Arctic Red River) – 6 August 2005," in *The Highway of the Atom*, 202.

61 I saw this on television, but the incident was also written up on the CBC News website. "Wandering Polar Bears a Sign of Climate Change: Expert," CBC News, April 3, 2008, http://www.cbc.ca/news/canada/north/wandering-polar-bears-a-sign-of-climate-change-expert-1.708529.

62 I looked at a number of survivalist websites and collected this material in 2008.

63 "Meet the Doomsayers of our Time," *Hamilton Spectator*, February 15, 2009, http://www.thespec.com/news-story/2084756-meet-the-doomsayers-of-our-time/.

64 Annie Dillard, *An American Childhood* (New York: Harper Perennial, 2008), 11.

65 Ami Chen Mills, "Breaking the Silence," *Metroactive*, December 12, 1996,

http://www.metroactive.com//papers/metro/12.12.96/cover/china1-9650.

66 Quoted in Chen Mills.

67 Jack Gilbert, "A Brief for the Defense," *The Sun* magazine, July 2013, http://thesunmagazine.org/issues/451/a_brief_for_the_defense.

68 Forgotten Voices, Living History: International Conference for Educators on the History of WWII in Asia, Ontario Institute for Studies in Education, University of Toronto, October 1–2, 2010, http://archive .alpha-canada.org/educonference/index.htm.

69 Erna Paris, *Long Shadows: Truth, Lies and History* (Toronto: Alfred A. Knopf Canada, 2000), 131.

70 Ibid.

71 Kenzaburo Oe, *Hiroshima Notes*, trans. David L. Swain and Toshi Yonezawa (New York: Marion Boyars, 1995), 19. Originally published as *Hiroshima Noto* (Tokyo: Iwanami Shoten, 1965).

72 Michael Cunningham. "Prisoners of the Japanese and the Politics of Apology: A Battle over History and Memory," in special issue, *Journal of Contemporary History* 39, no. 4 (October 2004): 565.

73 Abraham and Torok, 166.

74 Ibid., 171.

75 Kuniko Muramoto, "Trans-generational Transmission of Historical Trauma and Attempts for Reconciliation with the Healing the Wounds of History Method," in *International Seminar, Remembering Nanjing 2009: Generational Transmission of War Trauma and Efforts for Reconciliation*, ed. Kuniko Muramoto (Kyoto, Japan: Ritsumeikan University, 2010), 19, http://www.ritsumeihuman.com/hsrc/resource /19/open_research19_menu1e.pdf.

76 Quoted in Ruth Barcan, "Problems without Solutions: Teaching Theory and the Politics of Hope," *Continuum: Journal of Media & Cultural Studies* 16, no. 3 (2002): 343.

77 Adam Levy, "The Ground Zero They Didn't Want Us to See," *Guardian*, July 16, 2005, https://www.theguardian.com/theguardian/2005/jul/16 /weekend7.weekend2.

78 Wilfred Burchett, "Wilfred Burchett: The Atomic Plague," *Fair Ob-*

servor, August 27, 2014, http://www.fairobserver.com/region/north
_america/wilfred-burchett-atomic-plague-99732/.

79 Quoted in Bob Greene, *Duty: A Father, His Son, and the Man Who
Won the War* (Toronto: Perennial, 2001), 145.

80 Ibid., 45–46.

81 Kim Mackrael, "We're Sorry, Japanese Government Tells Canadian
POWs," *Globe and Mail*, December 8, 2011, http://www.theglobeandmail
.com/news/politics/were-sorry-japanese-government-tells-canadian
-pows/article554679.

82 Peter van Wyck, two emails to the author, June 10, 2014.

83 Quoted in van Wyck, *The Highway of the Atom*, 3.

84 Déline Dene Band Uranium Committee.

85 Van Wyck, *The Highway of the Atom*, 3.

86 Thich Nhat Hanh, "Please Call Me by My True Names," *The Path of
Compassion: Writings on Socially Engaged Buddhims*, ed. Fred Epp-
steiner (Berkeley, CA: Parallax Press, 1988).

JOURNEY OF THE MAGPIE:
A BIBLIOGRAPHIC ESSAY

Wandering through a tangled wood, I don't remember every source. I carry a pen, write everything down and collect. Images build into shapes, and eventually there are bits of paper all over my study. They start to form chapters. Then the chapters are torn apart and restructured.

It really did start with the phone call from Peter van Wyck. He had seen Peter Blow's 1998 film *Village of Widows*, which is essential viewing if you want to know more about Déline. As is the Déline Dene Band Uranium Committee's 1998 report, *They Never Told Us These Things*, and George Blondin's published work. Cindy Kenny-Gilday, who was a major force getting the Dene to Hiroshima, has an essay called "A Village of Widows." I recommend anything you can find by journalist Andrew Nikiforuk referencing Déline, including his 1998 *Calgary Herald* essay "Echoes of the Atomic Age."

I bought a big art book with blank pages and wrote headings: Déline, Apology, Witness, Secrets, Elegy, Haunting, Japan, Nuclear. It wasn't personal yet – there was nothing about my own life – just the issues that had concerned me, first as a theatre artist working with communities and then as a scholar. Some of the writers who helped most with that part of the book include: Teresa Simm, who wrote a beautiful paper as a graduate student about Japanese haunting and performance rituals to appease hungry ghosts; Nicolas Abraham and Maria Torok, early psychoanalysts whose book *The Shell and the Kernel* evokes intergenerational haunting; and

Jacques Derrida and his question, "How do we play the deadly serious game of living?" All my work as a graduate student with the late Roger I. Simon informs this book, as do conversations with colleagues from those years. It was in graduate school that I first developed the language of witnessing. Roger's published work on ethics, collective memory and what it means to take seriously the job of the witness is an invaluable resource. From those days, it was conversations with the late Sharon Rosenberg and her searing poetic scholarship that led to my conviction that horror is unbearable without beauty. Her photo was on my desk while I wrote this book.

When Juliet Palmer and I began dreaming up the opera *Shelter*, I became obsessed with nuclear scientists. Because details provoke my imagination, I read about weather, sandstorms and electricity, and went to talks by nuclear scholars and artists. Robert Jungk's engrossing *Brighter Than A Thousand Suns: A Personal History of the Atomic Scientists* brought to life the complexity and drama of the development of the bomb. When Peter and I went to Déline at the beginning of all this, I found *Great Bear: A Journey Remembered*, by Frederick B. Watt. I kept that book close and it inspired the first draft of *Shelter*.

For the first years, after the trips to Déline and New Mexico, I had no idea how to write about what I had experienced. I kept myself busy with the opera, but in the back of my mind were my notebooks and this huge story that I had expected to tell on stage but didn't. *Shelter* became a fable about the atomic age, the story of a couple that give birth to a radioactive child. The child's governess is the physicist Lise Meitner, and the man who steals her away is an atomic pilot. This tale took on a life of its own, while my travels on the atomic highway waited like a sulky teenager in the basement.

One evening, after a day at the Toronto International Festival of Authors, I was inspired to try my hand at fiction. I didn't know anything about writing short stories, so this felt safe; I didn't have to be any good at it. Each morning for a year, I wrote a paragraph or two; four stories later, my trip to Déline began to come alive on the page. Later, when I was looking for the details from my time up north, I found them hiding in my fiction.

In 2008, I brought my fragments of text to the Banff Centre to do a workshop with Myrna Kostash. I had heard Myrna speak in Toronto about something called "creative nonfiction," which seemed to fit the combination of imaginative thinking and real stories at the heart of my work with communities and the theatre. Myrna was the first champion of this project. Her unerring ear and passion for justice helped me see not only the story that needed telling, but also my way into that story. Myrna told me that this was a book. She also suggested that it was a memoir. "But I hate memoir!" I wailed. When she asked me why, I said it was confession that I hated. That realization, and Vivian Gornick's stunning guide to nonfiction writing *The Situation and the Story*, set me on my way.

Some of the most important books that guided me were either offered by friends and colleagues or discovered in bookstores and libraries. Priscila Uppal's *We Are What We Mourn: the Contemporary English-Canadian Elegy* helped me understand that I was writing an elegy. I almost called the book *An Atomic Elegy*, and I suggest Uppal's work to anyone interested in literature, mourning and memory. Don Gillmor, my wonderful editor from the Banff Literary Journalism program, loaned me his copy of Robert Jay Lifton and Greg Mitchell's *Hiroshima in America: Fifty Years of Denial*. That book (which I have not yet returned!) and Walter A. Davis's *Death's Dream Kingdom: The American Psyche Since 9-11* grounded the impressions I had about the relationship between personal turmoil, politics and the psychological anxieties of threat. Both books helped me to make sense of my own adolescence and the forces that shaped my impulse to activism. Erna Paris's *Long*

Shadows: Truth, Lies and History opened my eyes to the atrocities committed by the Japanese and took me to the 2010 conference on war crimes in Toronto.

Peter van Wyck's *Highway of the Atom* is a story of Déline, but it is also much more: a poetic philosophy and literary dreaming that follows the layers of a path that has no mappable geography. I didn't read Peter's book until I was finished writing my own, but we started doing public readings together and the text of this book grew in relation to Peter's voice, both on the page and in public. We still read this way, a kind of oral duet that makes it almost impossible for me to speak my own words without hearing his. Peter's contribution to this book, his earlier writing and his generosity in offering information, ideas and editorial support, is immeasurable.

I read several fine novels about the atomic age. Shaena Lambert's *Radiance* was one of my favourites, and it was Shaena who said that when I went to Hiroshima I must go somewhere beautiful. She suggested Miyajima. There are other writers who live permanently beside my desk. Annie Dillard, Tim Lilburn and Don McKay are only a few of the poet philosophers who have been my guides.

In 2011, South African poet and journalist Antjie Krog spoke at Kingston WritersFest. In *Begging to Be Black*, Krog describes a conversation with a philosopher in Berlin. She tells him what writing is for her:

> I explain to him that in order to understand something I have to write it; while writing – writingly, as it were – I find myself dissolving into, becoming towards what I am trying to understand.
>
> "Tracing the lines of flight is what Deleuze calls it." The professor is a translator of Deleuze's work.
>
> "I am not fleeing! This is why I am having this discussion. I'm staying, but I want to understand with what I am staying."

"Not flight as in fleeing, but flight as in going in a particular direction. One moves from an established known identity by transforming oneself. But transformation always moves in a particular direction and writing is often the best way to trace these directions."

And thus I had my title.

From the beginning, I received different feedback about how much Peter should be in the book. Readers of early drafts told me to take him out; it wasn't clear why he was in the story, particularly since he didn't accompany me to Japan. In the final stages of editing, Noelle Allen asked me to show a bit more of our relationship, how we talked and worked together. I asked Susan Olding about this. Susan's *Pathologies* had shown me how powerful the braided form of nonfiction could work in a book-length manuscript, and she had been a very helpful reader for an earlier draft of *Lines of Flight*. Susan sent me the following email, and a quotation from the Robert Pinsky translation of Dante's *Inferno*:

Peter needs to be there because he leads you into the darkness (learning more and more about the atomic mess we are in) but also to joy. If you are Dante, he is Virgil. That's the archetype.

> Midway on our life's journey, I found myself
> In dark woods, the right road lost. To tell
> About those woods is hard – so tangled and rough

Susan followed the quotation with this: "Dante would never have emerged from that wood without Virgil."

BIBLIOGRAPHY

Abraham, Nicolas, and Maria Torok. *The Shell and the Kernel: Renewals of Psychoanalysis*. Chicago: University of Chicago Press, 1994.

Avni, Ora. "Beyond Psychoanalysis: Elie Wiesel's *Night* in Historical Perspective." In *Auschwitz and After: Race, Culture, and "the Jewish Question" in France*, edited by Lawrence D. Kritzman, 203–18. New York: Routledge, 1995.

Blondin, George. *When the World Was New: Stories of the Sahtú Dene*. Yellowknife: Outcrop, 1990.

———. *Yamoria the Lawmaker: Stories of the Dene*. 1st ed. Edmonton: NeWest Press, 1997.

Bogdan, Deanne. "The Shiver-Shimmer Factor: Musical Spirituality, Emotion, and Education." *Philosophy of Music Education Review* 18, no. 2 (Fall 2010): 111–29.

Brugge, Doug, Timothy Benally and Esther Yazzie-Lewis, eds. *The Navajo People and Uranium Mining*. Albuquerque: University of New Mexico Press, 2007.

Chang, Iris. *The Rape of Nanking: The Forgotten Holocaust of World War II*. New York: Basic Books, 1997.

Cunningham, Michael. "Prisoners of the Japanese and the Politics of Apology: A Battle over History and Memory." Special issue, *Journal of Contemporary History* 39, no. 4 (October 2004): 561–74.

Cyrulnik, Boris. *The Whispering of Ghosts: Trauma and Resilience*. Translated by Susan Fairfield. New York: Other Press, 2010.

Davis, Walter A. *Death's Dream Kingdom: The American Psyche Since 9-11*. London: Pluto Press, 2006.

Felman, Shoshanna, and Dori Laub. *Testimony: Crises of Witnessing in Literature, Psychoanalysis, and History*. New York: Routledge, 1992.

Fitzpatrick, Blake. *Blake Fitzpatrick: Uranium Landscapes*. Peterborough, ON: Art Gallery of Peterborough, 1999.

Grace, Sherrill, Eve D'Aeth and Lisa Chalykoff, eds. *Staging North: Twelve Canadian Plays*. Toronto: Playwrights Canada Press, 1999.

Greene, Bob. *Duty: A Father, His Son, and the Man Who Won the War*. Toronto: Perennial, 2001.

Griffiths, Linda, and Maria Campbell. *The Book of Jessica: A Theatrical Transformation*. Toronto: Coach House Press, 1989.

Haley, John O. "Apology and Pardon: Learning from Japan." *American Behavioral Scientist* 41, no. 6 (March 1998): 842–67.

Jolly, Rosemary. *Cultured Violence: Narrative, Social Suffering, and Engendering Human Rights in Contemporary South Africa*. Liverpool: Liverpool University Press, 2010.

Jungk, Robert. *Brighter Than a Thousand Suns: A Personal History of the Atomic Scientists*. Translated by James Cleugh. New York: Harcourt, Brace and Company, 1958.

Kakuzō, Okakura. *The Book of Tea*. New York: Duffield, 1906.

Kenny-Gilday, Cindy. "A Village of Widows." In *Peace, Justice and Freedom: Human Rights Challenges for the New Millennium*, edited by Gurcharan S. Bhatia, J. S. O'Neill, Gerald L. Gall and Patrick D. Bendin, 107–18. Edmonton: the University of Alberta Press, 2000.

Lifton, Robert Jay, and Greg Mitchell. *Hiroshima in America: Fifty Years of Denial*. New York: Putnam Adult, 1995.

Lilburn, Tim. "How to be Here?" In *Living In The World As If It Were Home*. Toronto: Cormorant Books, 1999.

McNeley, James Kale. *Holy Wind in Navajo Philosophy*. Tucson: University of Arizona Press, 1981.

Muramoto, Kuniko. "Trans-generational Transmission of Historical Trauma and Attempts for Reconciliation with the Healing the Wounds of History Method." In *International Seminar, Remembering Nanjing 2009: Generational Transmission of War Trauma and Efforts for Reconciliation*, edited by Kuniko Muramoto, 14–21. Tokyo, Japan: Ritsumeikan University, 2010.

Oe, Kenzaburo. *Hiroshima Notes*. Translated by David L. Swain and Toshi Yonezawa. New York, London: Marion Boyars, 1995.

Oliver, Kelly. *Witnessing: Beyond Recognition*. Minneapolis: University of Minnesota Press, 2001.

Paris, Erna. *Long Shadows: Truth, Lies and History*. Toronto: Alfred A. Knopf Canada, 2000.

Parr, Joy. *Sensing Changes: Technologies, Environments, and the Everyday, 1953–2003*. Vancouver: University of British Columbia Press, 2010.

Rosenthal, Debra. *At the Heart of the Bomb: the Dangerous Allure of Weapons Work*. Reading, MA: Addison-Wesley, 1990.

Salverson, Julie. "Taking Liberties: a Theatre Class of Foolish Witnesses." *Research in Drama Education* 13, no. 2 (2008): 245–55.

———. "Witnessing Subjects: A Fool's Help." In *A Boal Companion: Dialogues on Theatre and Cultural Politics*, edited by Mady Schutzman and Jan Cohen-Cruz, 146–57. London and New York: Routledge, 2006.

Sanger, Penny. *Blind Faith: The Nuclear Industry in One Small Town*. Toronto: McGraw-Hill Ryerson, 1981.

Sime, Ruth Lewin. *Lise Meitner: A Life in Physics*. Berkeley: University of California Press, 1996.

Torpey, John. "Making Whole What Has Been Smashed: Reflections on Reparations." In *The Journal of Modern History* 73 (2001): 333–58.

van Wyck, Peter C. *The Highway of the Atom*. Montreal: McGill-Queen's University Press, 2010.

Village of Widows. Videocassette (VHS). Produced by Peter Blow. Peterborough, ON: Lindum Films, 1998.

wa Thiong'o, Ngũgĩ. *Decolonising the Mind: the Politics of Language in African Literature*. London: James Currey, 1986.

Watt, Frederick B. *Great Bear: A Journey Remembered*. Yellowknife: Outcrop, 1980.

Weart, Spencer. "Nuclear Fear." In *Filling the Hole in the Nuclear Future: Arts and Popular Culture Respond to the Bomb*, edited by Robert Jacobs. Lanham, MD: Lexington Books, 2010.

Wiebe, Rudy. *Playing Dead: A Contemplation Concerning the Arctic*. Edmonton: NeWest Press, 2003.

Wiesel, Elie. *Night*. Translated by Stella Rodway. New York: Hill and Wang, 1960.

JULIE SALVERSON is a playwright, librettist, scholar and non-fiction writer who teaches drama at Queen's University and the Royal Military College of Canada. She has published essays about the artist as witness, atomic culture, ethics and the imagination. Salverson has created projects in community-engaged arts practice for many years, and works with groups to practice resiliency through the exchange and development of stories. She is a member of the Playwrights Guild of Canada and her plays have been produced in Canada, the US and Thailand. Visit her website at https://jsalverson.wordpress.com/.